Behaviorspeak:

Glossary of Terms in

Applied Behavior Analysis (ABA)

Bobby Newman, Ph.D., B.C.B.A.
Kenneth F. Reeve, Ph.D.
Sharon A. Reeve, Ph.D., B.C.B.A.
Carolyn S. Ryan, M.A., M.Phil., B.C.B.A.

Dove and Orca

ISBN # 0-9668528-4-2

Dedications

This work is dedicated to Leo Newman, the best father a person could have. He spent decades working at a mind-numbing job that was beneath his abilities so that his children would have an opportunity for something better. Still, there was never a time he was too busy to play catch. There was never a question he wouldn't answer. If I asked him to pick up a particular book some time, he inevitably came off the subway with it the very next night. He took me to professional wrestling on school nights. He is a true role model who knows what is really important. I hope to be half the father he is. He reads children's books to his grandson as though they were written by Charles Dickens, and is such a great editor that he caught that we misspelled "Lawrence, KS" in the original reference section. As my co-authors all violated my wishes and mentioned me in their dedications, let me thank them for showing the rarest kind of loyalty and friendship over the years --- B. N.

My efforts on this book were supported in part by a faculty grant from Caldwell College. Gratitude is also extended to my earliest teachers, my parents, for consistently teaching me about ABA by applying it to my own emerging behavior. I would also like to thank my colleague Bobby Newman for his friendship throughout the years, and for his invitation to join this project. Lastly, I wish to acknowledge my wife, best friend, and colleague, Sharon, for all her love and support.
--- K. F. R.

First and foremost, I am grateful to all the individuals with autism and their families with whom I have had the pleasure of interacting with over the years. I am always inspired by their accomplishments. I'd also like to acknowledge all of my colleagues in the field of ABA, in education, and at Caldwell College, for sharing their expertise as to how to most effectively teach and apply behavior analytic principles. I, too, would like to thank Bobby Newman for his invitation to participate in this very fulfilling endeavor. Finally, my best friend and colleague is, coincidentally enough, also my spouse. Kenny has helped inspire me to become a better scientist, educator, and person. --- S. A. R.

My heartfelt gratitude and appreciation is extended to Bobby Newman for introducing me to the field of behavior analysis. This has led to countless rewarding opportunities, including this project. I am truly thankful to all of my professors, mentors, colleagues, and students from whom I've learned so much. I also acknowledge my sister Joyce for her endless encouragement, love, and support. — C. S. R.

Foreword

The purpose of this guide is to provide an "at your fingertips" reference to terms commonly used in Applied Behavior Analysis (ABA). In this way, parents, direct care providers, and others in the field of ABA will have an easily understood guide to answer the question, "what do behavior analysts mean by that?" Quite frankly, without a familiarity with some of the technical terms, understanding some practitioners of ABA is about as easy as trying to lip-read a muppet.

When I (BN) first started in this field, I was very fortunate to be surrounded by caring professionals who patiently explained each term to me, and then used the terms in everyday conversation in such a way that I soon learned what people jokingly call "behaviorspeak." Let's be honest, you don't hear many people outside the world of ABA talking about "in-your-seat behavior" and other similar terms. Never once have I heard, outside of ABA people, someone say "Good following directions!" Things that behavior analysts come to take for granted, in terms of speaking and thinking, are not second nature to everyone. This, then, is a guide for those who are not as fortunate as I was and who would like to learn the correct use of some of the terms. You certainly don't want to appear foolish at a cocktail party by confusing the use of "tact" and "mand," do you?

Throughout this book, an effort has been made to be technically precise. As in any science, ABA included, terms must be defined so that all involved are speaking the same language. When there was a choice between being technically precise and being understandable, however, we leaned towards the side of being understandable. We fully agree with Einstein (we think it was) who said: "Explanations should be made as simple as possible, but no simpler." We hope we didn't cross the line into watering things down. As we were writing this, we tried to keep the style of answering a question if someone were to ask, "what does *term x* mean?"

Please note that some terms are commonly used to refer to different, even if highly related, procedures. We have tried to be complete in such cases and give all usages. Unfortunately, there is a little Lewis Carroll in all of us. Sometimes we all use words to mean what we mean them to mean, regardless of what other people think. As I (BN) remarked in a previous work, I sometimes feel like a character in *The Princess Bride*: "You keep on using that word! I do not think it means what you think it means."

When using this glossary, please remember that sometimes terms mean something different in Applied Behavior Analysis than they do in everyday language, and sometimes they do not. As you Led Zeppelin fans will know, "sometimes words have two meanings." When a term required the use of another term, we capitalized the second term within the definition, cross-referenced for completeness. In the case of synonymous terms (e.g., "secondary" and "conditioned" reinforcers), the definition was simply repeated under both entries, with the appropriate wording changes.

As a final bit of advice, try to be technically precise when using these terms whenever possible. In this way, everyone in the field will be using the same language to communicate with one another. Bearing in mind the definition of "reinforcement" given in the book, for example, it is clear that you reinforce particular behaviors, not individuals. It is technically correct to say "I reinforced Tommy's initiation." It would not be technically correct to say "I reinforced Tommy." The same goes for other procedures. We extinguish behavior, for example, not individuals. That would be cruel and illegal.

We know that many of you are providing help to individuals diagnosed with autistic-spectrum disorders, so we threw in some of those terms as well. You can thank us later. In all seriousness, you are to be heartily commended for your work. As Vonnegut said, the meaning of life is to help each other get through this thing, whatever it is.

ABA Glossary

A CLOCKWORK ORANGE: Science fiction novel by Anthony Burgess that showed nightmarish uses of some BEHAVIOR MODIFICATION techniques. Misunderstandings about the book abound, due to the failure of U.S. publishers to include the last chapter of the book in its U.S. printings for over 20 years, and the failure of the popular movie to include this last chapter. The last chapter is crucial, as it changes the focus of the work from behavioral technology to more general morality and free will issues.

A.B.A.: An acronym that is used to refer to the field of APPLIED BEHAVIOR ANALYSIS, the application of the science of learning to socially significant human behavior. It is also the acronym used to refer to the professional organization dedicated to the field, the international Association for Behavior Analysis. You can find more information about the organization on the web at www.abainternational.org We suggest that you start attending the A.B.A. conference each year, it's the best way to stay current with the field. You would also get to attend the A.B.A. Social, a party at the end of the A.B.A convention each year. You haven't lived until you've watched all the top behavior analysts in the world getting down to *Dirty Deeds, Done Dirt Cheap.* You'll know what a day is, my friend.

A –> B –> C DESCRIPTION: A description of a RESPONSE in terms of the Antecedent (A), Behavior (B), and Consequence (C) of the response. An ANTECEDENT is the stimulus that immediately precedes the behavior. The BEHAVIOR is a description of the response in terms of its TOPOGRAPHY. The CONSEQUENCE is the immediate outcome of the behavior. Also called the THREE-TERM CONTINGENCY. Also a great song by the Jackson 5.

ABILITY: Refers to what an individual is *capable* of doing. This is sometimes used to contrast with PERFORMANCE, which refers to what an individual *actually does* on a given occasion.

ABLLS (THE): Acronym for the Assessment of Basic Language and Learning Skills, a language assessment tool in common usage within Applied Behavior Analytic programs. Created by Drs. James W. Partington and Mark L. Sundberg.

ACCOUNTABILITY: A very important component of ABA, this refers to the ethical principle that a treatment procedure must be demonstrated to be effective in order to be used. Such a demonstration requires an objective collection of DATA both before and after the implementation of the procedure, and its effect on the behavior in question. Objective data are required because this allows any individual so interested to assess the effectiveness of a treatment procedure, without the worry of having results clouded by personal bias or opinion. If Dr. Ego says that she is sure an intervention was effective, ask for the data that objectively demonstrates this effectiveness. Without such evidence, her confidence in the treatment is of limited use or value. See also DEMONSTRABLY EFFECTIVE and EMPIRICAL.

ACQUISITION: The time during which an individual is learning a new behavior. Data collected on the rate (speed) and accuracy of the skill being acquired informs the interventionist working with an individual as to whether the teaching procedures being used need to be adjusted.

ACTIVE STUDENT RESPONDING (LEARNING): A hallmark of all ABA instructional procedures, this is the requirement that students need to learn skills through interacting with their environment (e.g., teachers, instructional materials, etc.) as opposed to trying to learn by simply sitting back and observing or listening. Even though skills may be modeled for a child, or instructions may be presented, the child must demonstrate the skill (active responding!) to infer that learning has taken place. Active responding also allows the interventionist to determine the speed with which learning is occurring and whether adjustments need to be made in the intervention itself. (This is also the reason why those mean old teachers used to call on you in class!)

ACTIVITIES OF DAILY LIVING (ADL): This term refers to a myriad of behaviors involved in taking care of one's self (e.g., toilet usage, washing, dressing, eating, etc.). These behaviors are also referred to as SELF-HELP SKILLS. Also see VINELAND ADAPTIVE BEHAVIOR SCALES.

ACTIVITY REINFORCER: The individual earns access to a favored (more probable) activity by engaging in less favored (less probable) activities.   See also PREMACK REINFORCERS.   As with all other types of REINFORCEMENT, it is only a REINFORCER if CONTINGENT access results in an increase in the TARGET BEHAVIOR.   For example, Eddie is more likely to complete his homework because he is only allowed to play video games once the homework is done. For all you Pink Floyd fans out there, "How can you have any pudding if you don't eat your meat?"

ACTIVITY SCHEDULE: A procedure wherein individuals are taught to follow a series of written or pictorial cues, engaging in the BEHAVIOR CHAIN represented. The ability to follow such a schedule is an important one for many students with disabilities to learn, as this can increase independence and help the individual to learn to occupy leisure time ("down time") appropriately. A key component is to teach people to follow schedules in general, and not just to learn one particular schedule. See an excellent book by McClannahan and Krantz (1999) for elaboration.

AIR CRIB: A temperature and humidity controlled crib for human infants developed by B. F. SKINNER. It was developed to allow children freedom in the crib, without the need for heavy clothing and blankets. After its appearance in an article in *Ladies Home Journal* in the 1940s, a myth began that Skinner was conducting experiments on his children in such devices. This myth may have started because the magazine feature was called "Baby in a Box" and it was well-known at the time that Skinner actively researched learning by studying animals in devices called operant chambers or SKINNER

BOXES. This led to an unfortunate and corny joke on the part of those who did not understand the device. They called the cribs "heir conditioners."

ALTERNATING TREATMENTS DESIGN: This term refers to an EXPERIMENTAL DESIGN wherein during any given session, one of a specified number of experimental conditions will be in place. For example, one might be conducting a study of the effect of "Teaching Method A" versus "Teaching Method B". During randomly selected sessions (e.g., sessions numbers 1, 2, 5, 7, 8, 11, 12, 13, 17), Teaching Method A will be implemented. During the remainder of the sessions, Teaching Method B will be implemented. At the end of the experiment, results from the two teaching methods are compared.

ANALOGUE: A term referring to an attempt to recreate the real-life situation within the laboratory. Some functional analyses are conducted, for example, by "staging" typical situations within the laboratory. This is done in an attempt to determine the function of a behavior. For example, a student who engages in SELF-INJURIOUS BEHAVIOR might be exposed to high-demand, low-demand, CONTINGENT attention and EXTINCTION conditions in order to ascertain the FUNCTION of the behavior outside the laboratory setting.

ANTECEDENT: A stimulus that immediately precedes a behavior. The "A" in the THREE-TERM CONTINGENCY. Sometimes called a "PROMPT," although this may not be precisely correct according to some definitions of the term (see PROMPT).   Also see DISCRIMINATIVE STIMULUS.

APPETITIVE STIMULUS: This term refers to a reinforcing stimulus. See also POSITIVE REINFORCER.

APPLIED BEHAVIOR ANALYSIS (A.B.A.): The application of the science of learning to socially significant human behavior.

APPROXIMATION: This is a less-than-perfect attempt at a TARGET BEHAVIOR. Within the SHAPING paradigm, an approximation may either lead to reinforcement or be extinguished, depending on the current step (see SHAPING for elaboration). Within many programs, if a behavior is called an approximation, it is understood that this behavior will lead to reinforcement.

ARBITRARY MATCHING: In simple terms, teaching an individual that two or more seemingly unrelated stimuli "belong together." In such cases, there is no physical similarity among the items to indicate "belongingness." Rather, the belongingness is based on some arbitrary decision or verbal/written rule (This is in contrast to IDENTITY MATCHING). Arbitrary matching skills are often taught in word-object associations. For example, a child may be instructed to place a card with the written word "CAT" next to a picture of a cat.

A.S.A.T.: An acronym referring to the Association for Science in Autism Treatment. This organization works to support solid research regarding the autistic-spectrum disorders, and to ensure that only EMPIRICALLY VERIFIED and DEMONSTRABLY EFFECTIVE treatments are used when working with this clinical population. More information can be found at their web site, www.asatonline.org

ASCENDING: This term is used to refer to behavior that is increasing in value. Often used in analysis of behavior graphs, it refers to a behavior where the overall trend depicts increasing values of behavior (e.g., FREQUENCY, RATE, DURATION, PERCENT CORRECT, etc.).

ATTENTION-SEEKING BEHAVIOR: Behavior that has been determined through FUNCTIONAL ANALYSIS to be an attempt to get another individual to make personal contact. This may be appropriate (e.g., a verbal or nonverbal gesture that is culturally acceptable) or may be inappropriate (e.g., aggression or SELF-INJURIOUS BEHAVIOR). If inappropriate, this behavior is frequently the target of a BEHAVIOR TREATMENT PLAN. A frequently useful treatment plan in such cases is to identify FUNCTIONALLY EQUIVALENT behavior that can be taught so the person is able to seek out attention appropriately.

AUGMENTATIVE COMMUNICATION: This is an umbrella term for a variety of communication systems that are used to help individuals who are having difficulty acquiring spoken language. SIGN LANGUAGE, communication boards and the PICTURE EXCHANGE COMMUNICATION SYSTEM (P.E.C.S) are common examples. Augmentative communication systems are not intended to replace spoken language, but rather to supplement it to help an individual make his/her needs and thoughts known. A balance must be struck in formulating a strategy for the use of augmentative communication systems, as learning an augmentative communication system may reduce the need for an individual to learn spoken language. On the other hand, if an individual has no means of making thoughts and needs known, a great deal of inappropriate behavior that serves a communicative function may be observed.

AUTISTIC SPECTRUM DISORDERS (ASD's): This term generally refers to a class of developmental disorders typically appearing by age 3. ASD's include Autistic disorder (or Autism), Childhood Disintegrative Disorder, Rett's Disorder, Asperger syndrome, and Pervasive Developmental Disorder NotOtherwise Specified (PDD-NOS). The word "spectrum" refers to the idea that in each of these disorders, the adaptive functioning of the individual may range along a continuum (from low to high). Typically, skill levels are assessed for the following three major areas: (a) spoken and non-spoken communication skills, (b) social interaction skills, and (c) problems related to non-adaptive behavior (such as inflexibility and pre-occupations with repetitiveness). Autistic disorder, Asperger syndrome, and PDD-NOS are also part of a broader class of Pervasive Developmental Disorders (PDD), defined in the DSM-IV TR. The term "pervasive" implies that the effects of the disorder are observed throughout many aspects of the person's behavioral repertoire.

AUTONOMY: A general philosophical construct referring to the ability of the person to choose and engage in behavior. It is a common criticism made by those outside the field of ABA that somehow behavioral procedures reduce an individual's autonomy. In fact, the opposite is true. Applied Behavior Analysis teaches skills to individuals. If I do not have a skill, I do not have a CHOICE. I simply can't engage in the behavior if I don't know how. If someone teaches me a given skill, however, now I have a choice. I can engage in the behavior or not, at my discretion. Right now, I choose to stop defining "autonomy."

AVERSIVE: This is a stimulus that serves as a POSITIVE PUNISHER when immediately presented following a behavior (decreases the future probability of a given behavior), or whose removal serves as a NEGATIVE REINFORCER when removed following a behavior (increases the future probability of a given behavior). It is important to note that aversives are every bit as individual as REINFORCERS. What serves as a reinforcer for one student may serve as an aversive for another. Behavior analysts generally avoid the use of aversives, as they may lead to many "side-effects" (e.g., avoidance efforts by the student, counter-aggression, emotional responses, loss of staff reinforcer value, modeled use of punishment for interventionists). Aversives have also been referred to as "the dark side of the force" in that they can be temporarily quite effective and therefore quite seductive. For example, if a staff member delivers an aversive to a student engaging in severe SELF-INJURIOUS BEHAVIOR, this CONTINGENT aversive will likely reduce the SIB. The act of delivering the aversive by the staff member has therefore been

NEGATIVELY REINFORCED (remember that reinforcement does not only affect student behavior!). As a result, the staff member may therefore be more likely to use an aversive in the future for less severe behavior ("using the death penalty for murder AND jay-walking").

AVOIDANCE: A behavior whose function is to allow the individual to stay away from undesired settings or tasks. Although this term is frequently used interchangeably with ESCAPE behavior, escape technically refers to getting away from situations or tasks that have already begun, whereas avoidance refers to such behavior occurring prior to the undesired setting or task. NEGATIVE REINFORCEMENT generally maintains avoidance behavior.

BACKUP REINFORCER: This refers to some consequence that has already been demonstrated to reinforce an individual's behavior. Often, when backup reinforcers are presented in exchange for other stimuli, such as tokens, these new stimuli become reinforcing in their own right. For example, if a child must earn 10 tokens to receive the backup reinforcer of 10 minutes of video watching, the tokens will also become effective reinforcers. In this case, the tokens have become CONDITIONED REINFORCERS through their pairing with the original backup reinforcer (access to video watching). Also see GENERALIZED REINFORCER.

BACKWARD CHAINING: This is a specific method of instruction wherein one attempts to teach a task by teaching the last step first and working through a TASK ANALYSIS in reverse. This method of teaching has an advantage in that a student sees the "finished product" from the very beginning of the teaching process. When teaching a child to put on a shirt, for example, the interventionist might place the shirt on the student, and then teach the child to tuck it in. Once this is mastered, the interventionist would put the shirt on the student, but leave it halfway down the torso. The student would work on pulling the shirt down and then tucking it in. A third step might include the interventionist putting the shirt on the student, but leaving one arm out of a sleeve. Now the student must put the arm through the sleeve, pull the shirt down, and tuck it in. In this way, one would teach the student the entire BEHAVIOR CHAIN of the task, working from last step to first.

BACKWARD CONDITIONING: In the CLASSICAL CONDITIONING paradigm, presenting an UNCONDITIONED STIMULUS prior to the CONDITIONED STIMULUS. According to most research, this does not make for very effective learning. Would the word, "fore," mean anything to you if people only yelled it after a ball had already pelted your cranium?

BASELINE: This is a period of observation during which we gather DATA relevant to intervention. When conducting a FUNCTIONAL ANALYSIS, this might mean just measuring a behavior so as to ascertain its LEVEL and collecting A–> B –> C data, without engaging in specific interventions. When discussing teaching programs, the term "baseline" may refer to ascertaining student skill levels on specific programs so as to choose the proper starting points. Note that BASELINE is also sometimes incorrectly used as a verb (e.g., "I'm going to baseline his color identification program"). Baseline gives us a value to compare against. If you heard that a student hit himself ten times in a given day, is that good? It might not seem good on the surface, but what if he had hit himself 985 times the day before? Without a baseline to compare against, given measures of behavior may not be meaningful. Also see SINGLE-SUBJECT DESIGNS.

BEHAVIOR: This term refers to some action made by an individual. Within the RADICAL BEHAVIORISM paradigm, this behavior can be OVERT (publically observable movements through space) or COVERT (observable only to the person engaging in the behavior, such as thinking).

BEHAVIOR ANALYST: A person who practices the science of ABA. The initial training may have been in psychology, education, speech therapy, or some other related discipline. Important note: see also BOARD CERTIFIED BEHAVIOR ANALYST for a description of the credentialing process.

BEHAVIOR CHAIN: Multiple steps that make up a given behavior or activity. See CHAINING, TASK ANALYSIS and FORWARD and BACKWARD CHAINING.

BEHAVIOR GOAL: This is a statement of a target for behavior increase or decrease. It should include very specific descriptions of the following:

A. What behavior is under consideration?

B. How much of the behavior should be seen?

C. Under what circumstances should the behavior occur?

See also the DEAD MAN'S TEST.

BEHAVIOR MODIFICATION: This term is sometimes used interchangeably with ABA. Most practitioners of ABA avoid the use of this term, however, as it is associated with the use of aversives by some, and a belief that the term does not emphasize the *analysis of data* that is the hallmark of the discipline of APPLIED BEHAVIOR ANALYSIS.

BEHAVIOR SPECIFIC PRAISE: See TELEGRAPHIC PRAISE.

BEHAVIOR "TRAP": Refers to a situation in which an individual's behavior is maintained by its contact with reinforcers that are naturally produced by the emission of that behavior. For example, appropriate language use typically produces desired changes in the behavior of others: A child who can say "Mommy, please give me a snack" is likely to receive a snack. If a child is severely delayed in language use, however, the child is unlikely to experience the reinforcers typically produced by language use. To ameliorate this, a child may be formally taught to ask for many varied specific objects until this skill becomes generalized. Once this occurs, it is likely that this skill will be maintained through its being "trapped" by the natural contingencies of language production.

BEHAVIOR TREATMENT PLAN: This is a written description outlining how relevant individuals in a client's environment should respond if a given target behavior occurs, or if a given target behavior does not occur. The plan should specify exactly what behavior is under consideration, what the behavior treatment plan is called in the clinical literature, the rationale for choosing this particular technique versus other available techniques, any considerations or special information interventionists need to know that are particular to this individual, the data collection system, and when one should stop doing the plan (consider the goal mastered).

BEHAVIORAL DEFICIT: This is a general term that refers to the inability of a person to engage in behavior that typically developing people of his/her age can produce.

BEHAVIORAL EXCESS: This is a general term that refers to an individual engaging in behavior that typically developing people of his/her age do not.

BEHAVIORISM: The philosophy of the science of BEHAVIOR. It takes several forms, but always emphasizes that behavior is the proper subject matter of psychology and should be studied using an objective scientific, experimental methodology.

BEHAVIOROLOGY: A term used by some to refer to the science of APPLIED BEHAVIOR ANALYSIS. Advocates of the use of this term suggest that ABA has progressed sufficiently that it should be considered its own science, rather than as a sub-field of psychology or education.

BETWEEN-GROUPS DESIGN: This is a form of research wherein large numbers of subjects are divided into groups (e.g., an experimental group and a control group).   The groups each experience a different treatment (this is the INDEPENDENT VARIABLE manipulated by the experimenter). Some DEPENDENT VARIABLE is measured to ascertain the effects of the treatment. Note that this type of research is rarely used in applied behavior analysis, due to the need for FUNCTIONAL ANALYSIS. Suppose one wanted to test a treatment for SELF-INJURIOUS BEHAVIOR (SIB) based upon an AVOIDANCE hypothesis. Would the treatment be effective? It would probably only work with those individuals who were engaging in the SIB for avoidance reasons. In a large group, however, there is no telling how many of the individuals fit this description and therefore one might conclude that a very effective treatment was not effective at all. In fact, the treatment might lead to an increase in SIB in individuals who are engaging in the behavior for ATTENTION-SEEKING reasons, and one might erroneously conclude that a potentially useful treatment is actually harmful. It is for this reason that behavior analysts rely predominantly on SINGLE-SUBJECT DESIGNS in research.

BLOCK OF TRIALS: This is a term often used in DISCRETE TRIAL TEACHING; it refers to a set of attempts (trials) to teach or practice a given skill. It is important to note that a block of trials can consist of any number. There is no set reason to do a specific number of trials. (The only reason I know of to always do ten trials is the complete inability of many people to calculate percentages in other numbers, or a lack of knowledge about how to use a calculator- BN). It is important to note that with many skills, you will present a block of material in ISOLATION and a block of RANDOMIZED material being worked on during each session. It is also important to note that many students will demonstrate behavioral difficulties if one presents too many trials of the same skill in a row. (So don't be afraid to skip around in the book).

BOARD CERTIFIED BEHAVIOR ANALYST: This is a person who has satisfied all the requirements to acquire the "B.C.B.A." and can therefore call him/herself a Board Certified Behavior Analyst. Requirements include completing a prerequisite number of hours of University-level course work in the science of behavior, completing a period of internship under the supervision of a Board Certified Behavior Analyst, and passing the required written examination. To maintain certification once it is achieved, there are various continuing education requirements. There are currently two levels of certification, the Board Certified Behavior Analyst (B.C.B.A.) and the Board Certified Associate Behavior Analyst (B.C.A.B.A.). The exact requirements and most current information regarding how to become or locate a Board Certified Behavior Analyst are available through the Behavior Analyst Certification Board web site, at www.BACB.com.

BRAVE NEW WORLD: A novel by Aldous Huxley that portrayed

BEHAVIOR MODIFICATION as an evil tool of an oppressive government. Interestingly, in a less appreciated but equally well-written book, Huxley reversed himself. In *Island*, one of Huxley's last works, the same behavioral techniques are shown being used to encourage enlightenment and social progress. (Bet you didn't know that! And you thought we were just a set of pretty faces and athletic bodies!)

C.A.B.A.S.: Acronym for the Comprehensive Application of Behavior Analysis to Schooling. See the work of R. Douglas Greer and colleagues.

C.A.R.S.: Acronym for the Childhood Autism Rating Scale. This assessment tool is used to help identify, and collect data regarding the presence of autistic-spectrum disorders by giving a questionnaire to parents or caregivers. It assesses specific and measurable behavior deficits and excesses based on those described in the DSM. Similar to a related measure called the G.A.R.S. (Gilliam Autism Rating Scale).

CASE STUDY: A description of the background of a particular individual, usually used to assist in treatment decisions. Because much of the information obtained in a case study involves recollection, information may suffer from biases and inaccuracies. A case study is not to be confused with a SINGLE-SUBJECT EXPERIMENTAL DESIGN, which involves experimental research used to determine the effects of a treatment procedure on a person's behavior. Unfortunately, it should be noted that case studies are notorious for being very efficient at persuading people to believe in a given premise or theory (e.g., "You should give your kid secretin! My brother's mailman's niece's kid took it and now he's fine!"). In actual practice, however, case studies are notoriously vulnerable to CONFOUNDS and should not be the sole basis upon which treatment decisions are made. See ACCOUNTABILITY.

CATEGORY: A group of stimuli that share a common characteristic that defines them. Cars, buses, boats, etc. form the category known as "transportation," for example. Also see STIMULUS CLASS.

CHAINING: A teaching procedure wherein one attempts to link various simple individual responses together to make one, longer complex behavior. One talks of "chaining" the individual responses that make up "setting a table," for example. This can be done through FORWARD CHAINING, BACKWARD CHAINING or TOTAL TASK PRESENTATION, generally following a TASK ANALYSIS. It is important to note that when doing a CHAINING procedure, one does not work on just the most current step, but also on all the steps that precede it. For example, if one were trying to teach the alphabet through forward chaining, one would teach "A" until mastered, then "AB" until mastered, then "ABC" until mastered, etc. (all the way through and including the famous letter, "ellemenoh").

CHANGING-CRITERION DESIGN: This term refers to a form of SINGLE-SUBJECT DESIGN in which the different experimental "phases" consist of systematic changes in what is required for the target response (e.g., greater and greater FLUENCY in demonstrating a given skill). In everyday language, we allude to this whenever somebody "raises the bar."

CHILD STUDY TEAM: A group of individuals who construct and implement a student's INDIVIDUALIZED EDUCATION PROGRAM (I.E.P.) or I.F.S.P. (INDIVIDUALIZED FAMILY SERVICE PLAN). It includes all involved interventionists, school administrators, related services personnel, parents, and the student requiring the services (when age-appropriate).

CHOICE: In everyday use, this term refers to providing two or more alternatives to an individual. In programming, however, it highlights the fact that programming can be mutually agreed upon by interventionist and student. A student might be allowed to pick the order of programs to be worked on, or the stimuli used, etc. Some studies have shown that providing such choice decreases COMPETING BEHAVIOR.

CLASSICAL CONDITIONING: Also known as RESPONDENT CONDITIONING or Pavlovian Conditioning, in honor of Ivan Pavlov, who described and popularized the procedure. This is a form of learning in which a previously NEUTRAL STIMULUS takes on RESPONSE-ELICITING properties through pairing with another stimulus that already possesses response-eliciting properties. In the earliest Pavlovian experiments, the ticking of a metronome (neutral stimulus) took on response-altering properties by being paired in a SHORT DELAY conditioning paradigm with an UNCONDITIONED STIMULUS (meat). When the neutral stimulus takes on response-eliciting properties, we say that the neutral stimulus has become a CONDITIONED STIMULUS and classical conditioning has occurred. This is the process underlying everyday instances in which one thing becomes associated with another. For example, we ask you to just think about nails on a chalkboard (sorry!). Also see CONDITIONED REINFORCER.

COERCIVE PROCEDURES: Absolutely not advocated by ABA, these are the methods involved in changing an unfortunate person's behavior through severe punishment (such as physical pain), deprivation (such as withholding safety, food, rest, or comfort), and/or extremely powerful reinforcers that are not considered socially acceptable (such as allowing a person to skirt the law or acquire huge sums of money or power). On a smaller scale, coercive procedures may also involve preventing a student from being able to choose certain preferred activities and reinforcers. Coercive procedures are often depicted on a grand scale in films (such as A CLOCKWORK ORANGE) in which "brainwashing" is employed. Please do not confuse the use of coercive procedures with ABA. That would be like confusing the use of electricity to play an educational video for a child with using electricity to execute someone. See Murray Sidman's *Coercion and its Fallout*.

COMMUNICATION: Behavior whose function is the transmission of information from one individual to another (e.g., MANDING or TACTING wants or specific facts). May be verbal, written, symbolic, or gestural. Are we getting through out there?

COMPETING BEHAVIOR: Behavior that interferes with the learning process, or interferes with an individual's ability to function in a less restrictive environment. An individual who engages in SELF-INJURIOUS BEHAVIOR (SIB) that serves an AVOIDANCE function, for example, is engaging in a competing behavior. The SIB makes new learning difficult, and prevents the individual from functioning in the less restrictive environment.

COMTE, AUGUSTE: Philosopher and social activist whose writings regarding a science of behavior, and the use of this science for social progress, anticipated the work of later behavior analysts. Way to go, Comte!

CONDITIONAL DISCRIMINATION: Refers to a situation in which the role of one DISCRIMINATIVE STIMULUS depends (is conditional) upon the context. For example, if a child is presented with a card with the written word CAT and two comparison pictures of a cat and a dog, we can then reinforce the correct comparison selection. In a conditional discrimination, this would depend on the context for selection. If told to "pick the one that is opposite," then selecting the picture of the dog would be correct. If told to "pick the one that is the same," then selecting the picture of the cat would be correct. Also see MATCHING TO SAMPLE.

CONDITIONED REINFORCER: A reinforcer that was previously NEUTRAL, but has become a reinforcer through PAIRING with a previously-established reinforcer. Money becomes a conditioned reinforcer by being paired with the commodities it purchases. Interventionists may become conditioned reinforcers for their student's behavior, through being paired with other reinforcers (e.g., praise, tokens, favored activities, etc.). Also called a SECONDARY REINFORCER. Also see CLASSICAL CONDITIONING.

CONDITIONED RESPONSE: Within the CLASSICAL CONDITIONING paradigm, this refers to a behavior that occurs in response to a CONDITIONED STIMULUS. In the original terminology, a CONDITIONAL RESPONSE.

CONDITIONED STIMULUS: Within the CLASSICAL CONDITIONING paradigm, this refers to a stimulus that was previously NEUTRAL, but has taken on response-eliciting properties through pairing with an UNCONDITIONED STIMULUS. In the original terminology, a CONDITIONAL STIMULUS. Conditioned stimuli can be APPETITIVE or AVERSIVE.

CONFOUND: A flaw in an experiment that allows for more than one explanation of a treatment effect. An experiment is said to be confounded if all relevant variables are not CONTROLLED. If one begins a behavioral intervention at the same time that a drug treatment is begun, for example, it is not possible to say which might be responsible for behavioral changes. It might be one or the other, or a combination of the two treatments.

CONSEQUENCE: The specific immediate result of a given behavior. The consequence may or may not have behavior-altering properties. Types of consequences include POSITIVE and NEGATIVE PUNISHMENT and POSITIVE and NEGATIVE REINFORCEMENT, as well as NEUTRAL STIMULUS. Also see the THREE-TERM CONTINGENCY.

CONTINGENCY: An "if/then" statement that describes the cause and effect relation between a given behavior and the consequence of that behavior. If you engage in behavior "x," then you will receive consequence "y."

CONTINGENCY CONTRACT: A statement, often written, and agreed to by two or more parties (e.g., student and interventionist). This statement describes the behavior –> consequence CONTINGENCY.

CONTINGENCY-SHAPED BEHAVIOR: Behavior learned from actual experiencing of the consequences of a given behavior. Often contrasted with RULE-GOVERNED BEHAVIOR. See also INSENSITIVITY TO REINFORCEMENT.

CONTINGENCY-SPECIFYING STIMULUS: A spoken, signed, depicted or written description of the relationship between a particular behavior and the consequence of that behavior. This term is often used in discussions of RULE-GOVERNED BEHAVIOR. Also see

CONTINGENCY CONTRACT.

CONTINUOUS REINFORCEMENT (CRF): A SCHEDULE OF REINFORCEMENT wherein every instance of a target behavior is reinforced. In technical language, this could be called a FIXED RATIO 1 schedule. Although CRF is effective for teaching skills quickly, it is rarely used exclusively or for very long because it builds in little RESISTANCE TO EXTINCTION.

CONTROL: This term is used in several related ways, referring to a comparison that allows for pure experimental effects to be noted. One is said to "control" for extraneous variables when one has designed an experiment that eliminates the possibility that the other variables are affecting behavior. In a slightly different but related usage, in SINGLE-SUBJECT experiments each subject is said to serve as his/her own control by comparing levels of behavior during BASELINE and intervention. See also CONTROL GROUP and CONFOUND.

In behavior analysis, the term also refers to the notion that environmental events (ANTECEDENTS and CONSEQUENCES) can affect our BEHAVIOR and that we can identify these events and their effects. Control refers more broadly to finding out what variables affect other variables in our world. In other scientific disciplines, for example, we can ask what "controls" the flow of the tides, what "controls" the spread of bacteria, what "controls" the growth of cells in the brain? Thus, in behavior analysis and other scientific disciplines, we are simply identifying functional relationships. In fact, because any person involved with another person (spouse, parent, child, teacher, therapist, business managers, etc.) is likely to be interested in what makes themselves and others "tick," these individuals are interested in this notion of "control." Unfortunately, some individuals outside of the study of behavior analysis have misconstrued this meaning of "control" by implying that it has something to do with the identification of COERCIVE PROCEDURES such as those used in A CLOCKWORK ORANGE. Remember that such a devious practice is completely counter to the ethics and humanistic ideals of ABA. Also see PREDICTION AND CONTROL and FUNCTIONAL ANALYSIS.

CONTROL GROUP: In BETWEEN-GROUPS designs, this is a group of participants who receive some sort of placebo treatment. This allows the experimenter to determine if the INDEPENDENT VARIABLE is truly effective, or if there is some other, unaccounted for, variable.

COOKIE CUTTER: A highly insulting slang term used to refer to teaching programs that are not individualized. It implies that providers give each student the same teaching programs and behavior management strategies, regardless of student skills or FUNCTIONAL ANALYSIS. This approach is actually the antithesis of the individualized teaching and behavior management that characterizes ABA.

CORRELATION: A statistical measure of the degree to which two variables are related (vary together). It must be noted that correlation does not necessarily imply causation. The number of oranges and grapefruits grown each year is highly correlated, for example. Neither causes the other, of course. Both are dependent on other factors (e.g., sunshine, rainfall, lack of frost, etc.). Correlations vary between +1 and -1. The closer one gets to "1," either in the positive or negative direction, the stronger the co-varying of the two variables. The closer to "0," the weaker the co-variance. The sign does not indicate strength. A positive correlation indicates that the two variables rise and fall together, while a negative correlation indicates that one rises as the other falls.

COVERT BEHAVIOR: According to RADICAL BEHAVIORISM, this refers to behavior that is not accessible to another individual. This is often used to refer to internal states such as thoughts and feelings. An important aspect of radical behavioral theory is that these events are not considered any less lawful nor determined than more public behavior. That is, they are just as affected by principles of learning as are observable behaviors. See also PRIVATE EVENTS and OVERT BEHAVIOR.

CREATIVITY: From a behavior analytic perspective, the term means to behave in an original and productive manner. For example, a child may build a small person out of his set of blocks even though he has never been explicitly taught to do this particular activity. Traditionally, creativity referred to some mysterious inherent quality of a person that was often attributed to that individual's personality.

Research in this area, however, has shown that by teaching a person to engage in a variety of responses, "creative" behavior may increase. See GENERALIZATION.

CRITERION: Refers to the level of skill that is set as an objective for an individual's BEHAVIOR GOAL. A behavior is said to have "met criterion" when the individual has met that goal. For example, a child may be required to correctly name the parts of a human face for three different pictures of faces to meet criterion for that skill. Collecting regular data on a particular skill allows the practitioner of ABA to determine the progress towards the criterion set for that skill. See also BEHAVIOR GOAL and CHANGING-CRITERION DESIGN.

CUE: A stimulus that signals a behavior. Sometimes used synonymously with ANTECEDENT, PROMPT, DISCRIMINATIVE STIMULUS, INSTRUCTION, and other terms that refer to stimuli occurring before a behavior. Depending on the person using the term, the definition may or may not imply behavioral effects (i.e., some people only use the term if an effect of the stimulus can be demonstrated).

CUMULATIVE RECORD: A record of behavior as measured by a CUMULATIVE RECORDER. On the cumulative record, a flat line indicates a period of no performance of TARGET BEHAVIOR. The steeper the SLOPE of the line, the more the target behavior has been emitted.

CUMULATIVE RECORDER: A device used in basic research in the "old days." A pen rests on a paper that rotates through a machine on a consistent, regular interval. If the organism EMITS the target response, the pen jumps slightly. A CUMULATIVE RECORD is made, with a flat line indicating periods of no responding and sloping lines indicating periods of responding. The steeper the slope, the more rapid the responding. Today, most cumulative records are produced using computer software.

CURRICULUM: The skills and information one is teaching. Also used to refer to the bank of materials from which teaching programs are chosen.

DANA REINECKE, BCBA: Highly skilled behavior analyst and partner of Bobby Newman, Dark Overlord of ABA. Widely considered to be the second most tolerant woman in the world, directly after Terri Irwin (married to Steve Irwin, the Crocodile Hunter).

DATA: The plural of datum, these are pieces of information gathered to guide the decision-making process. ABA relies upon DATA-BASED DECISION MAKING. Teaching and behavior management programs are based upon information that is systematically gathered during the teaching/working process.

DATA SAMPLING: This refers to a process of gathering estimates of behavior through specific data collection strategies. See also PARTIAL-INTERVAL RECORDING and MOMENTARY TIME

SAMPLING. This is especially useful when one is trying to collect data on a given COMPETING BEHAVIOR while one is simultaneously trying to teach a separate skill.

DATA-BASED DECISION MAKING: A requirement of ABA, this refers to the fact that teaching and behavior management decisions are based upon information that is systematically gathered during the teaching/working process. Also see ACCOUNTABILITY.

DEAD MAN'S (PERSON'S) TEST: A guiding principle in the creation of BEHAVIOR GOALS and BEHAVIOR TREATMENT PLANS. It basically states that anything a dead person can do is not behavior. If a dead person could meet your behavior goal, it is not a good plan. Dead people, for example, do not get out of their seats. Therefore "not getting out of seat" fails the dead man's test. The dead man's test reminds us to emphasize the behavior that we want to see, not the behavior we don't want to see. We should always be looking to increase desired behavior, not emphasizing the decrease in inappropriate behavior. Toilet training, for example, generally begins with teaching the individual how and when to eliminate. If one only reinforces not having accidents, all one has done is taught the individual to hold it in. We cannot expect that just because a person knows what not to do, that (s)he will somehow spontaneously have knowledge of what (s)he should do instead.

DELAY OF REINFORCEMENT: This term is used in everyday conversation to refer to the ability of reinforcers that are not immediately presented following a target behavior to influence a student's behavior. For example, can a student tolerate a delay of reinforcement long enough to use a TOKEN ECONOMY? In reality, this is more often a matter of whether the stimuli (such as tokens and praise) are functioning as CONDITIONED REINFORCERS, and not a matter of whether a student can actually learn with delayed reinforcement. When initially teaching a new skill, however, it is preferable to use immediate reinforcement rather than delayed reinforcement. In this way, the student more easily learns the CONTINGENCY between the behavior and its consequence.

DEMONSTRABLY EFFECTIVE: Referring to procedures that can be, or have been, proven to be effective in systematically altering behavior within the context of controlled and properly designed research. See ACCOUNTABILITY and EMPIRICALLY VERIFIED.

DEPENDENT VARIABLE: This is the "outcome" measure in an experiment. In an experiment where two different teaching methodologies (INDEPENDENT VARIABLE) are contrasted, for example, the dependent variable might be speed of acquisition of the skill in question, or examination scores. Contrast with INDEPENDENT VARIABLE. See also INTERNAL VALIDITY.

DEPRIVATION: To increase the potency of a reinforcer by not delivering it to the individual for a time. For example, to make access to a favorite video game particularly reinforcing, one might limit access to the game. Only when a particular behavior goal is met (e.g., independently urinating in the toilet), might the individual have access to the reinforcer. If an individual has unrestricted access to a particular reinforcer, it is unlikely to be particularly potent when offered as a reinforcer. Contrast with SATIATION. See also ESTABLISHING OPERATION, and note that some theorists are beginning to use the term "motivating operation."

DESCENDING: Term used to refer to behavior that is decreasing in value. This is often used in analysis of behavior graphs, and would refer to a behavior where the overall trend was decreasing values of behavior (e.g., FREQUENCY, RATE, DURATION, PERCENT CORRECT, etc.).

DESENSITIZATION: A CLASSICAL CONDITIONING procedure used to increase the tolerance of a given individual for a previously aversive stimulus. Helping an individual learn to tolerate a stimulus that previously caused discomfort (for example, helping a student to learn to be able to wear a particular fabric that was previously not tolerated, or to tolerate sounds that were previously unbearable). See also SYSTEMATIC DESENSITIZATION and HABITUATION.

DETERMINISM: One of the most important philosophical aspects of ABA. This holds that behavior follows general rules and laws, and does not just occur randomly. The assumption of determinism underlies research that seeks to discover functional relations between specified environmental variables (ANTECEDENTS and CONSEQUENCES) and behavior.

DIFFERENTIAL REINFORCEMENT OF HIGH RATES OF BEHAVIOR (DRH): A particular type of intermittent schedule of reinforcement that is also a behavior management technique, particularly within the FLUENCY literature. When implementing a Differential Reinforcement of High Rates (DRH) of behavior schedule, reinforcement is only forthcoming if a certain minimum number of responses are EMITTED correctly within a period of time. For example, a student might earn a reinforcer only if a full mathematics work sheet of 20 problems is correctly completed within a specified period of time. This procedure is also used to refer to a behavior management strategy wherein a minimum INTER-RESPONSE INTERVAL must not be exceeded in order for reinforcement to be forthcoming. This behavior management strategy is used when a behavior is occurring, but needs to occur more frequently. (See the famous "Candy Factory" episode of *I Love Lucy* for a comedic representation of a DRH schedule gone afoul).

DIFFERENTIAL REINFORCEMENT OF INCOMPATIBLE BEHAVIOR (DRI): A behavior management strategy wherein a behavior that is physically incompatible with a TARGET BEHAVIOR is taught and reinforced. The response you are teaching and reinforcing should be impossible to perform simultaneously with the target behavior. Head-slapping is impossible while one is walking with hands in a jacket pocket for example, so one might teach walking with hands in pockets in an attempt to decrease this SELF-INJURIOUS BEHAVIOR (SIB).

DIFFERENTIAL REINFORCEMENT OF LOW RATES OF BEHAVIOR (DRL): This is a behavior management strategy used when one does not want to totally eliminate a given behavior, but does want to reduce the behavior's frequency. As with DRH, this is a particular type of intermittent schedule of reinforcement that is also a behavior management technique. When implementing a Differential Reinforcement of Low Rates (DRL) of behavior schedule, reinforcement is only forthcoming if a certain minimum number of responses are not EMITTED within a period of time. In other words, the INTER-RESPONSE INTERVAL must be at least as long as a specified value. An example might be a long car ride, during which a parent would only answer "are we there yet?" if it has been at least five minutes since the last time the question was asked. If the INTER-RESPONSE INTERVAL had not been at least five minutes, the question would be ignored and the timer reset.

DIFFERENTIAL REINFORCEMENT OF OTHER BEHAVIOR (DRO): A behavior reduction procedure wherein reinforcement is forthcoming if an individual engages in any behavior other than the TARGET BEHAVIOR for a specified interval. One first conducts a BASELINE to determine roughly how frequently the target behavior occurs. This tells the INTERVENTIONIST the length of the interval in which it is unlikely the behavior will be EMITTED. Once this is done, the procedure is implemented. If the specified interval passes without the target behavior occurring, the reinforcer is delivered. If the individual does engage in the target behavior before the interval ends, the timer is reset, effectively postponing reinforcement. Note: it is most important to reset the timer if the individual engages in the target behavior. Consider what would happen if you did not reset the timer. A person is on a five minute DRO for not hitting. At the one minute mark, she hits someone. If you do not reset the timer, what is the incentive not to keep pummeling her neighbors for the next four minutes? It doesn't matter whether she hits someone once or 10,000 times, it is the same result when the timer rings at the end of the interval. Therefore, make sure to reset the timer any time the target behavior occurs.

DIFFERENTIAL REINFORCEMENT OF ZERO RATES: A term synonymous with DIFFERENTIAL REINFORCEMENT OF OTHER behavior, used by people who aren't cool enough to say "DRO."

DIRECT INSTRUCTION: A form of teaching that is heavily based upon behavioral principles. Students are taught in groups that are made up of students at roughly the same academic level, there is scripted and fast-paced presentation of materials, students respond as a group as well as individually, and there is a very high degree of student-instructor interaction with error correction and positive reinforcement for correct responding. Similar to a PERSONALIZED SYSTEM OF INSTRUCTION, there is an emphasis on very well-designed and researched modules that students must master before moving on to the next level (see work by Engelmann and Carnine).

DISCRETE TRIAL TEACHING: Discrete trial teaching is the THREE-TERM CONTINGENCY (A --> B --> C) relationship as applied to teaching new skills. It is necessary because of the difficulties many people with disabilities have in learning information from the everyday environment. Each "trial" is a separate attempt to teach a new behavior or reinforce a previously learned behavior. It is not a "free-flowing discussion" such as might be used to teach a typically-developing student, it is distinct packets (ANTECEDENT and then BEHAVIOR and then CONSEQUENCE, A --> B --> C). There are several "styles" or approaches to doing discrete trial instruction. Two of the most common methods are ERRORLESS LEARNING and NO-NO PROMPTING. Regardless of teaching strategy, baseline all skills (used here as a verb). Check what the student can do and program accordingly in terms of what the student needs to learn to be able to successfully function in less restrictive settings. Remember that some behaviors are actually multiple concepts (e.g., "yes" and "no" for factual information versus preferences). As skills are learned in discrete trial, loose teaching should be used to foster generalization of responding. The goal of discrete trial teaching is to improve lagging skills. When the student no longer needs this intensive instruction, efforts should be made to normalize teaching and introduce peer group participation as soon as possible. Students who are only taught using the discrete trial method rarely generalize their skills to more everyday situations. The way discrete trial teaching is often conducted can be quite aversive (e.g., doing 10 trials in a row of the same step, only working face to face and knee to knee, using the same stimuli over and over, etc.). Discrete trial teaching should *not* be aversive to the student. Allowing students to have as much choice of reinforcers and programming as possible will make sessions more productive. Varying the teaching situation (e.g., location, teacher, stimuli) will make teaching more interesting and foster generalization. See also INSTRUCTION. (From *Graduated Applied Behavior Analysis*): In the popular mind, discrete trial teaching has BECOME applied behavior analysis. People think that discrete trial teaching is all there is to ABA, when in fact it is only one of its myriad techniques. Countless "programmers" roam the countryside and cities, offering discrete trial instruction to families of children with autism. These individuals frequently have very limited knowledge of the information that has preceded this, and their students suffer as a result. We hope no one using this manual will fall into this trap.

DISCRIMINATION: This is behavioral control based upon ANTECEDENTS. That is, an individual can determine differences between conditions. The person engages in a specific behavior under one condition, but not another. For example, an individual crosses the street when the signal flashes "walk," but not when "don't walk" is flashing. See also STIMULUS CONTROL and DISCRIMINATIVE STIMULUS. Contrast with GENERALIZATION.

DISCRIMINATION TRAINING: A teaching procedure wherein a student is taught what behavior should be EMITTED under specific conditions, but not under other conditions. See DISCRIMINATION.

DISCRIMINATIVE STIMULUS: An ANTECEDENT stimulus that signals that a particular BEHAVIOR will be reinforced. See also S^D. In more everyday terms, these are the CUES that tell us what we should be doing and when.

DISTANCING: A behavior therapy term based upon CLASSICAL CONDITIONING principles. When one distances, one attempts to separate a given behavior from the setting in which it generally occurs, in order to break conditioned relationships between the setting and a behavior. For example, an individual attempting to quit smoking might engage in distancing by only smoking in one corner of the house. In this way, (s)he would break any existing links between smoking and talking on the phone, or eating, or shooting pool, etc.

DISTRACTORS: This term refers to teaching stimuli that are presented to provide alternate, incorrect choices for a student. When implementing a RECEPTIVE color identification program, for example, a red crayon and a blue crayon might be laid on the table and the student asked to touch/point to/give me/show me the red crayon. In this case, the blue crayon is the distractor. Also see MATCHING TO SAMPLE.

DSM (DIAGNOSTIC AND STATISTICAL MANUAL): Manual published by the American Psychiatric Association that categorizes and provides diagnostic criteria for behavioral and psychological disorders. The book is periodically updated. At the time of the writing of this glossary, the current edition is the DSM IV-TR (Fourth Edition, Text Revision).

DURATION: A measure of the length of time engaged in a given behavior. One might measure the duration of a tantrum, for example, in seconds or minutes. It can also refer to the length of time of a stimulus presentation.

ECHOIC: From Skinner's VERBAL BEHAVIOR, the repeating of previously heard utterances.

ECHOLALIA: A language difficulty common to the autistic-spectrum disorders, as well as some other disabilities, echolalia refers to the tendency to repeat previously heard speech. This can be:

1. Immediate (you say "what color?" and the person immediately repeats back "what color?")

2. Delayed (the person repeats an utterance heard minutes, hours, days, weeks, months, or even years ago, as in the case of a student of mine {BN} who would randomly repeat lines from the movie, *The Godfather*). Important note: echolalia can be very misleading without careful observation. One might mistake an echolalic response for a more spontaneous statement. Sometimes the confusion can be added to by echoed statements that are context appropriate or specific (e.g., a student who falls down and immediately says "Barney, are you ok?"). Another important factor to note is that although echolalia may be quite inappropriate, it is also good "practice" for the student. A student who is echolalic is practicing moving his lips, tongue, air flow, etc. Compared to a student who does not make any speech sounds, the child who is echolalic is considerably ahead of the game in terms of learning

independent speech. (Please note that it is dehumanizing to refer to this behavior as "parroting." Only insensitive slobs use this term).

EDIBLE REINFORCERS: Food items that may be used as reinforcers for some persons. One common myth surrounding ABA is that edibles are the predominant reinforcers used in all treatment procedures with children. In actuality, when edibles are used, they are always paired with other more natural reinforcers such as verbal praise, attention, and tokens and are faded as the student acquires other reinforcers. See also PRIMARY REINFORCER.

ELICIT: A term generally used in discussions of CLASSICAL CONDITIONING or reflexive behavior. This term generally refers to behavior that is not considered under voluntary control. For example, for many of us, the term "tax audit" elicits a fear response!

E.L.I.J.A.: A parent/professional partnership (Empowering Long Island's Journey through Autism) that provides public education to better the lives of people diagnosed with autistic-spectrum disorders. Their web-page at www.elija.org is an excellent place to begin learning about the autistic-spectrum disorders.

EMIT: A term generally used in discussions of OPERANT CONDITIONING or voluntary behavior. This term generally refers to behavior that is under the control of its consequences. For example, a child playing a video game emits a mouse click to open a door to a secret treasure in the game.

EMPIRICAL: This is a term that refers to observable phenomena. Empirical phenomena can be seen and studied. The term is also used in terms of experimental outcome. To say "it's an empirical matter" means that the question could be answered by a well-designed EXPERIMENT. Also see COVERT and OVERT BEHAVIOR.

EMPIRICALLY VERIFIED: Means that a claim has been supported by well controlled research. See also DEMONSTRABLY EFFECTIVE, EXPERIMENT and SCIENCE.

EQUIVALENCE CLASS: This term refers to a type of CATEGORY or STIMULUS CLASS in which a set of perceptually dissimilar items occasion a common response. For example, the written word DOG, a picture of a dog, and the sound of a bark may all occasion the verbal label "doggy" by a child.

ERRORLESS LEARNING: This refers to a form of DISCRETE TRIAL TEACHING. In errorless learning, the student is not allowed to make a mistake on any given trial. If the student does not perform the behavior correctly or does nothing, (s)he is prompted to correctly perform the target response before a new trial begins. If possible, (s)he is prevented from making the incorrect response in the first place through careful prompting. This increases the probability that the student will have more opportunities to make a correct response and receive reinforcement.

ESCAPE: Behavior whose function is to allow the individual to get away from undesired settings or tasks (i.e., aversive stimuli or situations). Although often used interchangeably with AVOIDANCE behavior, escape technically refers to getting away from situations or tasks that are already present, whereas avoidance refers to such behavior occurring prior to the undesired setting or task. NEGATIVE REINFORCEMENT generally maintains escape behavior. (Ask yourself how long you engage in conversation with telemarketers!)

ESTABLISHING OPERATION: Sometimes abbreviated as EO, this term refers to an alteration in the environment that affects the power of other stimuli to serve as reinforcers and antecedent stimuli. While always considered an aspect of the behavioral system of thought, this term has been receiving increased attention and consideration within the last few years. The use of noncontingent reinforcement procedures and assessing density of reinforcement to ensure that staff themselves are reinforcers for the individual students would be examples of manipulating EO's. Food deprivation to ensure that food would serve as a reinforcer for a rat's behavior in an experimental chamber would be a simple laboratory example. This term is often placed "before" the THREE-TERM CONTINGENCY to remind us that behavior does not occur in a vacuum. While there is a technical difference, this term is used interchangeably by many people with SETTING EVENT. See also DEPRIVATION and SATIATION, and note that some theorists are beginning to use the term "motivating operation."

EXEMPLAR: In simple terms, the word refers to an example of some

CATEGORY or class. That is, the stimulus (or response) in question has a particular characteristic that it shares with other members. For example, an exemplar of the STIMULUS CLASS (CATEGORY) of "dessert" might be a bowl of ice cream. An exemplar of the RESPONSE CLASS "daily living skills" would be tooth brushing. An exemplar of "EDIBLE REINFORCER" might be a cookie (unless of course the child doesn't find cookies reinforcing!). To increase GENERALIZATION, a skill should be taught in the presence of many exemplars. For example, teaching a child to say "dog" in the presence of one dog may not result in the child correctly identifying other exemplars of what a dog is. Rather, teaching this verbal label in the presence of many dog exemplars should increase the likelihood that the child will be able to correctly identify many (or any) exemplars of what a dog is. Also see LOOSE TEACHING.

EXPERIMENT (EXPERIMENTAL DESIGN): A type of research activity that involves changing only one component of an individual's (or group of individuals) environment (called an INDEPENDENT VARIABLE) to see its effect on some specified behavior (called a DEPENDENT VARIABLE). This allows researchers and clinicians to identify the functional (causal) relationship between variables. If more than one component of an individual's environment is changed at the same time, it is impossible to determine a causal relationship (see CONFOUND and CONTROL). Principles of learning used in ABA are determined through research using experimental designs (see SINGLE-SUBJECT DESIGN).

EXPRESSIVE PROGRAMS: Term used to refer to teaching programs that require the student to communicate an answer. This can be through speaking, through SIGN LANGUAGE, picture symbols, or some other AUGMENTATIVE COMMUNICATION system. An example might be an "expressive color identification" program in which the student is shown a color and asked to identify it, either verbally or through one of the other methods mentioned above.

EXTERNAL VALIDITY: This term refers to the extent to which the results of a given experiment are valid for (can be generalized to) other people or conditions. If a particular treatment is effective for one child, will it be effective for others? In ABA, this is often determined by replication of the experiment.

EXTINCTION: To cease reinforcing a previously reinforced behavior to decrease the behavior's frequency. To effectively carry out this procedure, the reinforcer maintaining a behavior must be identified. What would be the extinction plan for a student dropping to the ground, for example? Would you pick the student up or not? We do not currently have enough information; we know the behavior but do not know the reinforcer. Is the reinforcer "avoiding interaction"? If so, one might pick up the student so that (s)he could not avoid interactions with those present. On the other hand, if the student is dropping to the ground because (s)he finds being picked up reinforcing, then the proper extinction plan would be to not pick the student up (as long as this procedure does not risk injury to the student). Notice that depending on the FUNCTION of the behavior, completely opposite treatment plans might be called for to carry out an extinction plan. Important note: when carrying out an extinction plan, one must plan for the occurrence of an EXTINCTION BURST.

EXTINCTION BURST: A reliable phenomenon, this refers to the tendency for behavior "to get worse before it gets better" when a previously reinforced behavior is no longer reinforced (see EXTINCTION).   During the burst, the behavior will *temporarily* increase in frequency, magnitude, and variability. If it is not possible to continue the extinction procedure to completion due to variations becoming dangerous or intolerable, then one *should not begin* the extinction plan.   Otherwise, one might inadvertently make the behavior worse than it had been previously.

FACILITATED COMMUNICATION (FC): Originally proposed as a technique to assist people with severe developmental disabilities to communicate by providing physical support (usually HAND OVER HAND) as they type out messages on a keyboard. Although there was a great deal of initial excitement surrounding FC in the developmental disabilities community following anecdotal reports of its effectiveness in "opening the door" to individuals with severe disabilities, FC has since been discredited following controlled double-blind EXPERIMENTS. Not to be confused with AUGMENTATIVE COMMUNICATION. See the chapter by Gina Green (1996) for further details.

FADING: This term refers to gradually removing any extra PROMPTS one has introduced into a teaching situation. If one has engaged in STIMULUS SUPERIMPOSITION, for example, one needs to gradually remove the superimposed stimulus and fade back towards normalcy. The same could be said for HAND-OVER-HAND prompting, which might be gradually reduced by PROMPTING further and further up the arm, or more and more softly on the hand. Visual prompts might be faded by making the stimulus smaller and smaller, verbal prompts by introducing longer and longer time delays between an asked question and a supplied answer, etc. Think of fading as the gradual removal of "hints" that are no longer needed. Anyone remember how our parents faded out the PROMPTS when we were learning to ride a two-wheeler?

FAILURE TO GENERALIZE: The tendency of some individuals to learn under a particular set of circumstances, and then fail to be able to demonstrate the same skill when even minor changes occur in the environment (e.g., a student diagnosed with autism who learned to TACT while a teacher wore glasses, and then could not perform the same skill when the teacher took her glasses off). See also DISCRIMINATION, EXTERNAL VALIDITY, GENERALIZATION and LOOSE TEACHING. This problem is often ameliorated through the use of multiple teaching EXEMPLARS. See the landmark work of Stokes and Baer (1977).

FALSIFIABLE: This term refers to the fact that findings in science should be able to be proven wrong, if indeed they actually are incorrect. Every concept or finding is open to check and scrutiny.

For example, for years it was widely held and accepted that autism was caused by emotionally distant mothers (called "refrigerator mothers"). This belief said that because the children of such mothers felt emotionally rejected and abandoned, they then turned away from a desire to interact with others, thereby unconsciously choosing to become autistic. Scientific research into the causes of autism, however, has shown this view to have no validity at all. When ideas such as this are shown to be incorrect (falsified) by science, they are discarded and are replaced by more valid ideas. It is only through this process that we can learn the most accurate information. Remember that a person's belief in information does not necessarily make it so. To use one of BN's catch phrases, "30 years of garbage treatment is still garbage" (we cleaned it up a bit). In science, beliefs must be EMPIRICALLY VALIDATED. In contrast to the falsifiable "refrigerator mother" concept, consider "creation science."   This concept fails the falsifiability test and should more properly be called "creationism." Creationism is not a science, as it holds a central doctrine as unquestionably true (i.e., that the world was created in six days by a deity). Any empirical findings that disagree with this central tenet must be explained away or ignored, and thus creationism fails as a science.

FEEDBACK: This term refers to any stimulus that provides an individual with information regarding his/her past performance (e.g., anything from a staff performance evaluation to praise delivered to a client, or a correct MODEL of a given behavior following an inaccurate performance). Feedback can be affirmative or can provide correction.

FIXED INTERVAL SCHEDULE OF REINFORCEMENT: A particular type of INTERMITTENT SCHEDULE OF REINFORCEMENT wherein reinforcement is available for the first target response that occurs after a specified time interval has elapsed. A Fixed Interval 5 minute schedule, for example, indicates that the first response that occurs after five minutes have elapsed will be reinforced. Note that it does not matter how many responses occur during the interval itself, the only one that will be reinforced is the first one following the end of the interval. The behavior of turning on the television to watch "Brady Bunch" will not be reinforced until you turn on the TV at the time the show is being broadcast, for example. (Don't sneer: you know you loved that show!) See also SCALLOPING.

FIXED RATIO SCHEDULE OF REINFORCEMENT: An INTERMITTENT schedule of reinforcement that describes a CONTINGENCY such that emitting a specific number of a targeted response leads to reinforcement. In a common laboratory example, a rodent family member (rat) would press a bar five times and this would lead to the delivery of a food pellet. This would be described as fixed ratio 5 schedule (FR 5). Tony Orlando and Dawn described an FR 3 schedule in a popular song ("knock three times on the ceiling...").

FLOODING: Often used in terms of phobic behavior, flooding refers to exposing the individual to an overabundance of that which is feared. This is in contrast to the much more preferred strategy of

SYSTEMATIC DESENSITIZATION, wherein the effort is made to introduce the individual to the feared stimuli in slow increments.

FLUENCY: This general term refers to the ability of an individual to complete a given number of RESPONSES accurately within a given period of time

FOXX, RICHARD M.: The ultimate behavior analyst.

FREE OPERANT: This term refers to behavior that occurs freely in a given setting, without any specific CUE. A rat is placed in an operant conditioning chamber (a "Skinner Box"). He can press a bar as often as possible for REINFORCEMENT, without any specific cue needed to occasion the behavior. Contrast this with more of a DISCRETE TRIAL methodology such as would be seen if the rat were put in a maze. A trial begins when the rat is placed in the maze, and terminates when he reaches the end of the maze. A new trial would begin when he was placed at the starting gate once again. For another example, consider a typical classroom setting. Free operant behavior might include spontaneous sharing during snack time, or making an initiation to a peer during free play at recess. In contrast, a discrete trial might consist of a student raising a hand and answering a question in response to a teacher's question. Contrast with DISCRETE TRIAL TEACHING.

FREE WILL: The philosophical idea that individuals choose their behaviors at all times. Skinner and the behavior analysts upset many individuals by suggesting that human behavior was determined by genetics and environmental conditions.   Such individuals interpreted the behavioral concept of DETERMINISM as a challenge to the concept of free will and AUTONOMY.   Also see CHOICE, COERCIVE PROCEDURES, CONTROL.

FREQUENCY: Refers to the sheer number of target responses counted. For example, "the student made seven initiations to his peers." Note that this is related to RATE of response, which is frequency during a specified length of time (e.g., the number of vocal requests or "MANDS" in an hour).

FORWARD CHAINING: A type of chaining procedure in which the first step in a TASK ANALYSIS is taught first, then the second step, then the third step, through to the final step (the full behavior chain being emitted).   See also CHAINING and TASK ANALYSIS.

FUNCTION OF BEHAVIOR: Generally speaking, the variable maintaining a given behavior (e.g., what might be reinforcing the behavior?). Common functions of behavior include ACTIVITY REINFORCERS,   ATTENTION-SEEKING,   AVOIDANCE, COMMUNICATION, EDIBLE REINFORCERS, ESCAPE, TANGIBLES, SENSORY REINFORCERS.

FUNCTIONAL ANALYSIS: One of the central processes of ABA, functional analysis involves the steps taken to answer the central question of "why is he DOING that?" Note that the question is *not* "why did he start?" Sometimes behavior can start for one reason, but then continue on for other reasons. To be more scientific about it, we would state the question as "what are the variables maintaining behavior now?"

Step 1

Define the behavior in such a way that everyone can agree when it has happened and when it has not.

Step 2

Establish an appropriate measurement system for the behavior in question (e.g., frequency, rate, percentage, latency, magnitude, duration, etc.)

Step 3

BASELINE: observe the behavior under a variety of conditions to get a level for comparison purposes and collect A--> B --> C   Data (Antecedent --> Behavior --> Consequence)

Step 4

Draft a hypothesis regarding the variables controlling behavior based upon what is observed during baseline, particularly the A –> B –> C analysis.

Step 5

Test your hypothesis by carrying out the treatment plan logically suggested by your hypothesis. If it does not work, reassess. Did you carry out the plan improperly, or is it the wrong plan? Back to step three. Note that the different functions a given behavior might serve call for diametrically opposed treatment plans. If one believes SELF-INJURIOUS BEHAVIOR to be ATTENTION-SEEKING, one would not approach an individual who was engaging in SIB. In contrast, if a student is engaging in this behavior for AVOIDANCE reasons, one would not take a backwards step away from a student while the behavior was occurring. As Sherlock Holmes summarized in *A Scandal in Bohemia:* it is a capital mistake to formulate theories before one has all the available facts. One winds up twisting new facts to meet old theories, rather than old theories to meet new facts.

FUNCTIONAL EQUIVALENCE: Teaching a new behavior that serves the same purpose as another behavior. This is often used as a behavior replacement procedure, particularly with students who would be characterized as having communication deficits. For example, a student might be engaging in self-injurious behavior for ATTENTION-SEEKING reasons. In order to reduce this behavior, one might teach a more socially appropriate attention-seeking response (e.g., tugging on a staff member's sleeve).

G.A.R.S: Acronym for the Gilliam Autism Rating Scale. See the entry for the similar C.A.R.S. (Childhood Autism Rating Scale) for a description.

GENERALIZATION: Speaking broadly, generalization refers to variation in either response or setting. Response generalization refers to the student changing the form of a given behavior that serves the same function (e.g., saying "hi" as a greeting instead of "hello"). Stimulus generalization refers to the student engaging in a given behavior under conditions different than those used during teaching (e.g., saying "dog" in the presence of a new dog in the neighborhood).

Note that some conditions, e.g., the autistic-spectrum disorders, are often characterized by reduced probability of generalization across responses or settings. How to help individuals to learn to generalize must be a focus of any well-designed program. See also LOOSE TEACHING, DISCRIMINATION, EXEMPLAR, GENERALIZED SETTINGS, STIMULUS CONTROL, RESPONSE CLASS, MAINTENANCE. See Stokes and Baer (1977) for a classic reference.

GENERALIZED IMITATION: The RESPONSE CLASS of imitation. A person is said to demonstrate generalized imitation when (s)he imitates actions or sounds the first time (s)he observes them, without any prior training with these particular behaviors. This is a very important skill that helps to foster learning.

GENERALIZED REINFORCER: A sub-type of CONDITIONED REINFORCERS. These are reinforcers that can be exchanged for other reinforcers. These reinforcers are particularly powerful in that they can be traded in for a variety of reinforcers and are therefore less susceptible to the effects of DEPRIVATION and SATIATION than other types of reinforcers. See also TOKEN ECONOMY. (Check your wallet to see some great generalized reinforcers.)

GENERALIZED SETTINGS: Settings other than those where teaching has been conducted. Teaching or PROBING skills in generalized settings is a crucial aspect of GENERALIZATION.

GRADUATED APPLIED BEHAVIOR ANALYSIS: This term refers to the idea that programming and behavior management strategies must be altered in keeping with the functioning level of the student. A student might begin needing intensive 1-to-1 instruction and behavior management, but with appropriate learning will transition into less restrictive environments with typically developing peers. Teaching and behavior management strategies must change and become more normalizing as the student moves through the education experience.

GRAPHING: The representation of behavioral data on a grid. Various forms of Cartesian line graphs and STANDARD CELERATION CHARTS are in common use by behavior analysts. Graphs make for easy summarization of trends and level in behavior. They are used to assess progress in learning and to make teaching/treatment decisions.

GROUP-ORIENTED CONSEQUENCES: An arrangement in which contingencies are experienced by all members of a group, but are not based upon the behavior of all members (e.g., in American football, where the whole team is penalized five yards due to a rule infraction by one member). This is not recommended in clinical situations in which individuals cannot follow this complex relationship. When one student behaves inappropriately, the appropriate behavior of another student is not reinforced, and may even be punished. The student with a severe developmental delay may not understand why. Other higher-functioning students may observe a fellow student behaving inappropriately and realize that reinforcers will therefore not be forthcoming.   As they "sink or swim" as a team, the incentive for appropriate behavior by the other individuals is lost in such a situation.   There is no reinforcer for behaving appropriately while other students are behaving inappropriately.

HABITUATION: A decrease in response to a particular stimulus, as a result of repeated exposure to the same stimulus (e.g., people who live close to the railroad who cease to notice the sound of the trains). See also DESENSITIZATION.   In everyday language, considered the opposite of SENSITIZATION.

HAND-OVER-HAND PROMPT: Sometimes abbreviated HOH, this refers to providing physical guidance by placing an interventionist's hand over a student's hand, and guiding the student through the performance of a given behavior.

HUMANISM: A philosophical position, with roots in the Renaissance, that discounts supernatural explanations and holds science and human reason as the ultimate level of analysis.   The position is entirely consistent with APPLIED BEHAVIOR ANALYSIS. It should be noted that "third force" psychologists began using the term "humanistic" to refer to their approach during the second half of the twentieth century.   The third force approach, which was frequently anti-scientific, is actually not entirely consistent with the earlier philosophical tradition of humanism.

IDEA (INDIVIDUALS WITH DISABILITIES EDUCATION ACT): This law provides for and guarantees a free and appropriate public education (FAPE) for children identified as having special needs (e.g., autism, mental retardation, hearing or visual impairment, speech or language impairments, specific learning disabilities, etc.). Central to this goal is the development of an INDIVIDUALIZED EDUCATION PROGRAM (I.E.P.) for each child identified as having special needs.

IDENTITY MATCHING: In simple terms, teaching an individual that two physically identical stimuli "belong together." (This is in contrast to ARBITRARY MATCHING). Because identity matching skills are typically the easiest matching skills to learn, they are often taught prior to other types of matching.

I.E.P.: see INDIVIDUALIZED EDUCATION PROGRAM. Also see INDIVIDUALIZED FAMILY SERVICE PLAN (I.F.S.P.).

I.F.S.P.: see INDIVIDUALIZED FAMILY SERVICE PLAN. Also see INDIVIDUALIZED EDUCATION PROGRAM.

IMITATION: To copy observed actions or sounds. Most often discussed in ABA programming in terms of motor (a.k.a. nonverbal) imitation of actions, or verbal (a.k.a. vocal) imitation of speech sounds. Also see GENERALIZED IMITATION.

IMPULSIVITY: When faced with a choice, impulsivity refers to the tendency to engage in a behavior that produces a more immediate (but smaller) reward as opposed to engaging in a behavior that will produce a more delayed (but larger) reward. This is the opposite of SELF-CONTROL. For example, a child might choose an activity that produces 1 minute of opportunity to view a video immediately as opposed to choosing an activity that produces 10 minutes of video watching one 1 hour from now.

INCIDENTAL TEACHING: Generally speaking, incidental teaching refers to teaching that "takes advantage" of naturally occurring opportunities to teach, often with student-initiated activities. In clinical usage, this is often used when discussing GENERALIZATION training, with skills being practiced with stimuli "accidentally" encountered in GENERALIZED SETTINGS (actually pre-arranged conditions).

INCLUSION: Inclusion refers to the general philosophy of education that states that most, if not all, students with disabilities will spend all, or the majority of their time (in school or elsewhere), participating with their typically-developing peers. This term is often used interchangeably with MAINSTREAMING, but generally refers to a much broader, and possibly social, effort. These terms will be used differently by different people, however, with reference being made to:

1. how much time the student spends with typically developing peers,

2. how close (s)he is to typically developing peers behaviorally and academically,

3. how much support is needed, etc.

Understandably, this is a highly charged political area in educational policy discussions.

INCOMPATIBLE BEHAVIOR: Refers to engaging in one behavior that does not allow the possibility of another behavior to occur at the same time. Usually this would refer to instances in which a child learns to produce a more desirable behavior that precludes the option of engaging in the other less desirable behavior. For example, eating an apple is incompatible with aggressive biting; using a fork is incompatible with eating with one's fingers. See DIFFERENTIAL REINFORCEMENT OF INCOMPATIBLE BEHAVIOR.

INDEPENDENT VARIABLE: This is the variable manipulated by the researcher in an experiment. In a study of the effectiveness of a particular drug, for example, the independent variable might consist of receiving the drug or receiving a placebo. In a study of two different teaching methodologies, the independent variable would consist of which teaching methodology was received. Contrast with DEPENDENT VARIABLE. See also INTERNAL VALIDITY and EXPERIMENT.

INDIVIDUALIZATION: One of the hallmarks of ABA, this refers to designing teaching programs only after conducting a BASELINE of student skills, and designing behavior management strategies only after completing a FUNCTIONAL ANALYSIS. In any ABA program, a student's programs should only be based upon assessments conducted with that student. Contrast with COOKIE CUTTER programs.

INDIVIDUALIZED EDUCATION PROGRAM (I.E.P.): Each child (up to age 21 by Federal law) that receives special education and related services as a result of a disability is required, by law (see IDEA), to receive an Individualized Education Program (I.E.P.). This document lists specific educational goals and objectives for the child and describes the educational services that will best achieve them. Each I.E.P. is a collaborative effort of the CHILD STUDY TEAM (teachers, school administrators, related services personnel, parents, and the students themselves, when age appropriate). If not provided in some school systems, parents should be aware that they may need to formally request that a provision for ABA services be included in their child's IEP. Also see INDIVIDUALIZED FAMILY SERVICE PLAN.

INDIVIDUALIZED FAMILY SERVICE PLAN (I.F.S.P.): Similar in some ways to an I.E.P., this document is used to describe and guide early intervention services for children with disabilities aged 0-3 and their families. Guaranteed by law under the Individuals with Disabilities Education Act (see IDEA), the I.F.S.P. identifies and describes the services needed to enhance each individual child's development. It also identifies and describes any services that would enhance the family's ability to help the child achieve developmental objectives. Family members and service providers jointly determine how to best plan, carry out, and evaluate the services. Also see INDIVIDUALIZED EDUCATION PROGRAM.

INDIVIDUALLY BASED CONTINGENCIES: An arrangement whereby specific contingencies are based upon the behavior of a specific individual. This is the usual arrangement in ABA. Contrast with GROUP-ORIENTED CONTINGENCIES.

INHIBITORY STIMULUS: An ANTECEDENT that leads to a decrease in the probability of a behavior being EMITTED. For example, an "out of order" sign on a soda machine decreases the probability that a thirsty person will put money in the machine. This term can also be used in a CLASSICAL CONDITIONING paradigm to refer to CONDITIONED STIMULI that lead to suppression in responding.

INSENSITIVITY TO REINFORCEMENT: From RULE-GOVERNED BEHAVIOR research, the tendency of some individuals to follow verbal descriptions of contingencies, even when these descriptions are inaccurate. For example, a person told (s)he would be receiving reinforcers based on a FIXED RATIO schedule, when in fact the actual schedule was FIXED INTERVAL, nonetheless showed responding much more characteristic of fixed ratio schedules. A RESPONSE CLASS of "instruction-following" is theorized to be so powerful that it overcomes the effects of the actual reinforcers in place. This effect is most pronounced when reinforcers are highly delayed, when schedules of reinforcement are very lean, or reinforcers are of low potency. A good real-world example can be seen in people who carry rabbit feet for good luck because they are told to do so by another person. Notice that the foot wasn't particularly lucky for the rabbit!

INSTRUCTION: An ANTECEDENT stimulus, often verbal, that

directs an individual to engage in a given behavior. This may or may not include a description of the consequence one will receive for the given behavior. In DISCRETE TRIAL TEACHING, it is particularly important to note what instructions are being provided so as to maximize chances for GENERALIZATION. If a student always hears "point to" in a RECEPTIVE drill, he is unlikely to be able to perform the same skill when he hears "show me" or "touch" or "give me" or "which one is?". Make sure to vary these instructions so as to avoid dependence upon a particular phrasing. See also RULE-GOVERNED BEHAVIOR and CONTINGENCY-SPECIFYING STIMULUS, as well as CUE, PROMPT, DISCRIMINATIVE STIMULUS.

INSTRUMENTAL LEARNING: A term that is used synonymously with OPERANT CONDITIONING, this refers to learning based largely on the relationship between behavior and the consequences the behavior produces. See also CONTINGENCY, REINFORCEMENT, PUNISHMENT.

INTER-OBSERVER AGREEMENT: The degree to which two independent observers report the same results when observing a given behavior. A useful practice to ensure that interventionists are carrying out procedures consistently, IOA should be conducted periodically. Used synonymously with INTER-RATER RELIABILITY.

INTER-RATER RELIABILITY: See INTER-OBSERVER AGREEMENT.

INTER-RESPONSE TIME/INTER-RESPONSE INTERVAL: This refers to the amount of time in between target responses by the student. Often an object of analysis in Differential Reinforcement of Low rates (DRL) and Differential Reinforcement of High rates (DRH) procedures. (Your mom was concerned with your eating inter-response time when she said "Stop eating so fast! You're not being raised in a barn!")

INTER-TRIAL INTERVAL: This refers to the time between the end of one trial (generally a student response or corrective feedback) and the beginning of the next trial (the presentation of the S^D) by the interventionist. Also see DISCRETE TRIAL TEACHING.

INTERMITTENT REINFORCEMENT: Reinforcing only some instances of a given behavior, but not each time the behavior occurs (contrast with CONTINUOUS REINFORCEMENT). Generally speaking, intermittent reinforcement leads to behavior that is more resistant to extinction (e.g., think about why you continue to put money into a slot machine even if it doesn't pay off each time, but stop very quickly when a soda machine does not give you the soda you expect after putting your money in). This is important when teaching a new skill, as one would not want this skill to extinguish if reinforcement did not occur continuously. When teaching a desired behavior, one should try to change over from continuous to intermittent reinforcement as soon as possible to build in resistance to extinction. One can base intermittency on time (interval) or the number of responses (ratio). Requirements can be the same each time (fixed) or change (variable). A knowledge of intermittent reinforcement is also crucial when considering behavior that is targeted for reduction. If one reinforces screaming on the part of a child by allowing the child to avoid a task even every once in a while, that is intermittent reinforcement of screaming behavior (you have just become a slot machine). The student never knows when screaming will "pay off" and tends to engage in the behavior for a much longer time than if the behavior had been continuously reinforced and then extinguished. How is the student even supposed to realize that the behavior is on extinction if it has been intermittently reinforced? Maybe this is just one of those times when you're holding out, and maybe you'll eventually give in and reinforce the screaming just like those other times. He may as well keep at it. See also FIXED and VARIABLE RATIO and FIXED and VARIABLE INTERVAL SCHEDULES OF REINFORCEMENT. (Notice that in our "dating rituals," playing "hard to get" tends to keep the interested pursuer interested. Can you guess why?)

INTERNAL VALIDITY: This term refers to the "tightness" of a given experiment, the extent to which it is free from CONFOUNDS. A study is said to have a high degree of internal validity when a clear statement can be made about the impact of the INDEPENDENT VARIABLE on the DEPENDENT VARIABLE. Also see EXPERIMENT.

INTERVENTIONIST: Generic term for anyone carrying out behavior management and teaching procedures (teachers, teacher assistants, speech therapists, parents, occupational therapists, behavior analysts, etc.).

INTRAVERBAL: From Skinner's *Verbal Behavior,* a verbal response that is controlled by the verbal responses of others. A program wherein a student "fills in" a missing word would be an example of an intraverbal: "Twinkle, twinkle, little _____."

INTRINSIC VS. EXTRINSIC REINFORCEMENT: Generally seen as the distinction between engaging in an activity for "the fun of it" (intrinsic reinforcement) as opposed to receiving a tangible discrete reinforcer for engaging in the activity (extrinsic reinforcement). This distinction, however, may be less real than the definition would suggest, as many prior extrinsically reinforced behaviors come to appear to be intrinsically reinforced over the course of learning. For example, a child may initially receive edibles for attending to an adult. As the number of opportunities for other activities and more "natural" reinforcers (such as games and social interactions) increases through engaging in this attending behavior, the child will now attend without the edibles. The attending behavior now appears to be intrinsically motivated (see BEHAVIOR TRAP). It should be noted that there is a mistaken, but widely held, belief that using extrinsic reinforcers somehow lowers the intrinsic reinforcement value for a given activity or commodity. According to this reasoning, for example, if you pay a child to play with a favorite toy and later stop paying him to play with it, then he will no longer wish to play with the toy. Experiments have proven this belief to be inaccurate. Any suppression in a favored activity following cessation of extrinsic reinforcement is temporary, if it occurs at all. In other words, if the activity was fun in the first place, the person will return to the activity sooner rather than later. See articles by Cameron and Pierce, as well as Eisenberger and Cameron, in the references section.

ISOLATION: In DISCRETE TRIAL TEACHING, this refers to working on a skill separately from all others. When doing color identification, for example, a BLOCK OF TRIALS in which white was the correct choice each time might be conducted. It should be noted that many students can "over-learn" a single response when material is presented in isolation (e.g., touching head each time any body part is requested in a RECEPTIVE body part identification drill following isolated "head" trials). For this reason, some programs now advocate always introducing two steps simultaneously as this will decrease the probability that a student will over-learn a single response. It should also be noted that when single steps are introduced in isolation, it is possible that students appear to possess skills that they do not. Careful examination of the responding demonstrates that the student always needs to be PROMPTED on the first trial, but then gets all the remaining trials correct. This student has not learned the skill, (s)he has learned to keep repeating whatever step was prompted initially.

JABA: Pronounced "job ah," this is the acronym for the *Journal of Applied Behavior Analysis.* This is the journal for research in applied behavior analysis. Also see JEAB.

JEAB: Pronounced "jay ab," this is the acronym for the *Journal of the Experimental Analysis of Behavior.* The journal deals with laboratory research regarding basic principles of learning and behavior. Many of these principles form the basis of ABA when applied to socially significant behavior. Also see JABA.

JOINT ATTENTION: Refers to two individuals sharing an experience. This term is often used in discussions of individuals with socialization difficulties. The ability to say or respond to, for example, "look at that!" and share an experience with another individual is assumed to be crucial for social development. See also SHARING EXPERIENCES.

KELLER, FRED S.: Very popular and influential educator and philosopher of education. He created the behaviorally-based PERSONALIZED SYSTEM OF INSTRUCTION, and was a life-long advocate of DEMONSTRABLY EFFECTIVE education. See his paper "Good-bye, Teacher" and (with J. G. Sherman) *The PSI Handbook*.

LATENCY: A behavioral measure referring to the length of time required for a behavior to occur following a specific stimulus (e.g., latency to hanging up coat upon entering the classroom, or latency to covering ears in an overstimulating environment, or latency to saying "hi" when encountering a friend).

LEARNING: Relatively permanent changes in behavior that come about as result of experience with one's own actions in particular situations and the consequences they produce. Also seen as the ability to adapt to one's environment in a productive way. Principles governing learning are typically discovered, explained, and applied through the use of experimentation in behavior analysis.

LEAST RESTRICTIVE ENVIRONMENT: This refers to the most normalized environment in which a student can make academic and social gains. What is defined as the least restrictive environment is a very controversial area, with decisions having to be made regarding the importance of academic functioning, social functioning, impact on other students, etc. The goal of any educational program is to help the student to become ready to function and make gains in the least restrictive environment possible.

LEAST RESTRICTIVE TREATMENT MODEL: This is an ethical stance subscribed to by behavior analysts. It refers to the general principle that one does not implement a more AVERSIVE procedure before experimentally demonstrating that all less aversive and more reinforcing procedures have been attempted and proven ineffective for addressing the behavior in question.

LEAST-TO-MOST PROMPTING: This term refers to a PROMPTING and PROMPT FADING strategy wherein the interventionist begins with the lowest level of prompting possible (e.g., a very light arm tap) and builds in intensity if the student requires more aid to complete the task. In more general terms, the INTERVENTIONIST uses smaller "hints" unless larger ones are needed.

LEISURE SKILLS: Blanket term referring to behavior a person engages in "just for fun," or for recreation. When designing programs for individuals with developmental disabilities, the importance of leisure skills cannot be minimized, and we recommend working on these at the earliest opportunity (e.g., block building, coloring, computer games, even watching a video or listening to music appropriately). Remember the DEAD MAN'S TEST. Just because you have eliminated an inappropriate behavior does not mean that an appropriate behavior will spontaneously arise in its place. Leisure skills are normalizing in several respects:

A. Learning leisure skills allows the person to be appropriately and constructively engaged when not involved in active programming (see INCIDENTAL TEACHING). A person who does not possess adequate leisure skills may engage in inappropriate behavior during "down time."

B. They provide skills that can easily be turned into social activities.

C. They provide gist for conversation in social programs.

D. A person who does not possess leisure skills may appear much lower-functioning than (s)he actually is.

LEVEL: This term is often used in the analysis of data in graphs, and refers to how much of a given behavior is occurring.

LONG-DELAY CONDITIONING: Within the CLASSICAL CONDITIONING paradigm, this refers to a PAIRING arrangement such that the CONDITIONED STIMULUS is present for some long period of time prior to the introduction of the UNCONDITIONED STIMULUS. This is generally not as effective as SHORT-DELAY conditioning for teaching an individual to respond to the CONDITIONED STIMULUS, even though both procedures feature an overlap of CS and US.

LONGITUDINAL STUDY: A particular type of research wherein a given sample of individuals is followed for a very lengthy period of time (generally months, years or decades). This research is often used to assess long-term effects (MAINTENANCE) of earlier treatment/teaching procedures and to track developmental trends.

LOOSE TEACHING: This refers to a GENERALIZATION training procedure in which all non-essential aspects of the teaching situation are varied. One alters the time of day teaching occurs, place of teaching, teacher, phrasings, teaching stimuli, clothing worn, etc. Used to counter problems related to OVER-SELECTIVITY.

LOVAAS: The proper surname of O. Ivar Lovaas, clinician and researcher. His ground-breaking work using ABA with children with autistic-spectrum disorders (e.g., the 1987 study describing the Young Autism Project) has been so influential that some people outside the field refer to intensive ABA-based interventions for people with autism as "Lovaas therapy" or as "doing Lovaas."

MAGNITUDE: This is a measure of the intensity of behavior. Examples include the loudness of verbalizations and force of motor responses.

MAINSTREAMING: Refers to the general effort to help students with disabilities to participate in school or other activities with their typically-developing peers. This term, often used interchangeably with INCLUSION, is also often used to refer to a more piecemeal approach. These terms will be used differently by different people, however, with reference being made to:

1. how much time the student spends with typically developing peers,

2. how close (s)he is to typically developing peers behaviorally and academically,

3. how much support is needed, etc.

Understandably, this is a highly charged political area.

MAINTENANCE: Refers to the retention of learned skills over time. Also refers to procedures whose purpose is to ensure that skills that have been acquired are not lost. This may take the form of additional periodic practice sessions or the building of older programs into newer programs (e.g., one step direction programs that are built into "Simon Says" programs). Also referred to by some individuals as "GENERALIZATION across time."

MALOTT, RICHARD: Doctor Cool. Read his books and articles and watch his videos to see what we mean.

MAND: From Skinner's *Verbal Behavior* book, it means to request. One mands, for example, when one requests reinforcers. This takes several forms. The final goal in programming is generally the "pure" mand, which is a request that comes without any prompting from other individuals.

MASSED PRACTICE: This term is often used in discussions of DISCRETE TRIAL TEACHING. After a number of trials in which the student does not respond appropriately, sometimes "massed practice" is conducted where the student is led through the drill repeatedly until (s)he begins to demonstrate the skill independently. The student is prompted immediately on every trial. This is not always recommended, as it can be aversive. Sometimes also called mass trialing.

MASTERY CRITERIA: Refers to the conditions under which we call a skill mastered. In DISCRETE TRIAL TEACHING, for example, one might set a mastery criterion at 90% accuracy or above, across three consecutive sessions (for STABILITY) and across at least two INTERVENTIONISTS (for GENERALIZATION).

MATCHING TO SAMPLE: Refers to a teaching procedure in which some stimulus is presented (the sample) and a child must select the correct matching object from a set of comparison selections. The "rule" that describes a correct match may take many forms. Matching may be based on IDENTITY, as in the case when a child selects a red ball from the comparison choices when a red ball is held up as a sample. Matching may also be based on an ARBITRARY rule, as in the case when a child is taught to select a quarter from the comparison choices when a card with the written word "quarter" is presented as a sample. (Also see CONDITIONAL DISCRIMINATION)

MAURICE, CATHERINE: Author and activist whose writings and lectures sparked a major burst of interest in behavior analysis applied to the autistic-spectrum disorders, a burst that seems destined to be permanent.

MEAN: Another name for a numerical average. For example, a child emitted a mean of 7 social initiations on each day observed. Contrast with RANGE.

MEDICAL MODEL MYTH: Refers to the notion that non-productive or inappropriate behaviors seen in an individual are just symptoms of some hidden underlying cause that must be "uncovered" to effectively treat the individual. For example, when the study of autism was in its infancy, various practitioners incorrectly believed that the behavioral characteristics seen in children with autism actually reflected an underlying unconscious choice to turn away from the world because of a perceived emotional rejection by their mother. Practitioners of ABA, however, focus on the behaviors themselves rather than assuming there must be some hidden cause. See also SYMPTOM SUBSTITUTION.

MENTAL RETARDATION: Using DSM IV-TR criteria, this general diagnostic category refers to an individual who has three characteristics:

A. Intellectual functioning two standard deviations or more below the mean (on many common tests, a score of 70 or below).

B. Significant adaptive living skill deficits that make it difficult for the person to function independently in the world, given expectations for his/her age.

C. Onset before 18 years of age.

METAPHYSICAL BEHAVIORISM: An extreme subset of BEHAVIORISM, this philosophy held that mental states and feelings were a by-product of the functioning of the central nervous system and were not highly important to consider in understanding human behavior.

METHODOLOGICAL BEHAVIORISM: A subset of BEHAVIORISM, this philosophy holds that mental phenomena do exist, but they are outside the realm of public observation and therefore outside the realm of science.

MODELING: This term refers to demonstrating a behavior for an individual. This is often done in imitation training. It is also used in some clinical applications. A person with a phobia might be shown another individual interacting with their phobic stimulus, for example. In the latter usage, see the work of Albert Bandura and VICARIOUS REINFORCEMENT.

"MODIFIED" ABA: This is an attempt to combine bits and pieces of ABA with other approaches. This is no longer ABA. Anyone who says differently is selling something. Would you care to have an operation at a hospital that used "bits and pieces" of standard sterilization procedures?

MODULE: This term refers to a previously prepared unit of instruction, a skill that must be mastered before one moves on to learn future skills.

MOMENTARY TIME SAMPLING: A DATA SAMPLING procedure wherein time is broken up into specific intervals. The observer records whether or not a specific target behavior occurs at a specific moment (e.g., the first second of each 30 second interval). A percentage measure of the number of intervals in which the behavior was observed at the moment of observation is derived. This type of data collection can provide a good estimation of the incidence of a given behavior, but may also slightly underestimate incidence of behavior.

MOST-TO-LEAST PROMPTING: This term refers to a PROMPTING and PROMPT FADING strategy wherein one begins prompting at a level guaranteed to get the response to occur (e.g., a HAND-OVER-HAND PROMPT). One then FADES the intensity of the PROMPT over time to avoid PROMPT DEPENDENCY.

MOTIVATION: Loosely, this term refers to the "desire" an individual has for a given consequence. More specifically, an individual is said to be motivated for a given reinforcer when (s)he will engage in specified behavior to obtain the reinforcer. This term has been emphasized by those who stress NATURAL ENVIRONMENTAL TEACHING. As motivation can be a difficult issue with students diagnosed with particular disorders (e.g., the autistic-spectrum), we should take advantage of naturally occurring reinforcers and therefore motivational states. Rather than work on nonsense syllable production in VERBAL IMITATION, for example, we would attempt to have the student APPROXIMATE a MAND that would lead to the delivery of the reinforcer manded for. We may also manipulate ESTABLISHING OPERATIONS to increase motivation.

MULTIPLE-BASELINE DESIGN: An EXPERIMENTAL DESIGN in which BASELINE is begun simultaneously across conditions (behaviors, students, settings, etc.). Baseline is terminated and treatment introduced at different points across these conditions ("legs"). If behavioral changes occur only at the point at which treatment is introduced, one can conclude that the treatment is indeed the controlling variable (see INTERNAL VALIDITY). Along with REVERSAL DESIGNS, one of the most common research methodologies in ABA. Also see SINGLE-SUBJECT DESIGN.

NATURAL ENVIRONMENTAL TEACHING: Sometimes abbreviated as NET, this term refers to a teaching approach wherein the child's current activities and interests determine teaching strategies. It is often contrasted with DISCRETE TRIAL TEACHING, and emphasizes such factors as the child's motivational state, is "looser," and stresses naturally-occurring reinforcers. Although some people use the term INCIDENTAL TEACHING interchangeably with NET, the term incidental teaching is also used in everyday conversation to refer to a more DISCRETE TRIAL methodology, but within GENERALIZED SETTINGS. Also see INDIVIDUALIZATION.

NEGATIVE: In technical "behaviorspeak," refers to CONSEQUENCES involving the *withdrawal* of a stimulus, as in NEGATIVE REINFORCEMENT and NEGATIVE PUNISHMENT. The key is that the term "negative" is not a value judgement, but rather a description of a behavior –> consequence relationship (e.g., if you drive through the red traffic light, they will take away some of your money, or your driving privileges).   See CONTINGENCY.

NEGATIVE PRACTICE: A behavior-reduction procedure wherein an individual repeatedly performs an inappropriate behavior (s)he has EMITTED. This is often counter-indicated and should be undertaken only if suggested by a thorough FUNCTIONAL ANALYSIS and in keeping with the LEAST RESTRICTIVE TREATMENT model.

NEGATIVE PUNISHMENT: A CONTINGENCY wherein a particular stimulus is withdrawn following a given target behavior, and this leads to a decrease in the future probability of that target behavior. As with other consequences, it is important to remember that a stimulus is only a NEGATIVE PUNISHER if its contingent withdrawal leads to a decrease in the future probability of the behavior. If, for example, a child's favorite toy is removed following aggressive behavior, it is likely that the aggression will decrease in probability in the future.

NEGATIVE REINFORCEMENT: A CONTINGENCY such that the removal of a stimulus is contingent upon the EMITTING of a particular behavior. As with other forms of reinforcement, negative reinforcement leads to an *increase* in the future probability of a given behavior. Also as with other forms of reinforcement, the definition makes reference only to what actually occurs, not what one intends. AVOIDANCE behavior, for example, is often inadvertently maintained by negative reinforcement. A student tantrums in response to a request, and the interventionist withdraws the request as a result of the tantrum. In such a case, the interventionist has accidentally negatively reinforced the tantrum and unwittingly made it more likely in the future. Very sad! Please note that uninformed individuals often confuse this term with PUNISHMENT. Also very sad!

NEUTRAL STIMULUS: Within the CLASSICAL CONDITIONING paradigm, an antecedent stimulus that has no behavior ELICITING effect. Within the OPERANT CONDITIONING paradigm, a stimulus that has no behavior-altering properties when used as a CONSEQUENCE. It should be noted that a stimulus may start as neutral, but take on response-altering properties through subsequent learning. Ask yourself if money always meant something to you.

NONCONTINGENT: This term means that there is no systematic relationship between BEHAVIOR and CONSEQUENCE. This can sometimes be done as a PAIRING procedure, for example to pair a trainer with reinforcement. The interventionist would deliver reinforcers, no matter what the student's behavior, so as to establish the staff member as a CONDITIONED REINFORCER. This can also be done as a specific behavior treatment plan, attempting to break the relationship between an inappropriate behavior and a consequence. If it is determined, for example, through a FUNCTIONAL ANALYSIS that a student is running away in order to obtain food, one might deliver food noncontingently to eliminate the need for the inappropriate behavior. When parents or educators are told to "be consistent" with teaching, they are actually being told to "be contingent." The more noncontingent, generally the worse the learning. Unfortunately, many individuals confuse this idea with UNCONDITIONAL POSITIVE REGARD.

NONVERBAL: An adjective used to characterize individuals who do not speak, or to describe skills that do not require EXPRESSIVE skills.

NO-NO PROMPTING: This refers to a form of prompting within DISCRETE TRIAL TEACHING. In no-no prompting, a reinforcer is delivered if a student complies with a request following the first CUE. If the student does not accurately perform the skill, however, the student is led through a three-stage process. After the first incorrect response (or no response) the therapist says "no" and turns her head slightly. The CUE is given again. If the student again does not perform the response correctly, the therapist again says "no" with the head turn. After the third CUE, if the student does not perform the response correctly (s)he will receive a physical PROMPT. Note that sometimes interventionists substitute "nope" or other "softer" variations for "no" (but it's tough to say "nope-nope prompting").

NORMS: Refers to skill levels that the average individual should have achieved at a particular age. Often determined through STANDARDIZED TESTING.

OMISSION TRAINING: A term synonymous with DIFFERENTIAL REINFORCEMENT OF OTHER behavior, used by people who aren't cool enough to say "D.R.O."

OPERANT CONDITIONING: A type of learning that emphasizes the consequences of specific behavior as controlling variables for future occurrences of that behavior. One of the basic underpinnings of ABA. Also see INSTRUMENTAL LEARNING, CONTINGENCY, REINFORCEMENT, PUNISHMENT.

OVERCORRECTION: This term refers to a set of behavior-reduction procedures wherein an individual must correct the environmental impact of their inappropriate behavior, and often must practice appropriate behavior. A student who has thrown food down, for example, might be required to clean up the food (s)he has thrown down, as well as clean up the surrounding area (often a much larger area than was actually disturbed by the food-throwing).

OVER-SELECTIVITY: Often used in discussions of the autistic-spectrum disorders, this term refers to the tendency of an individual to notice only one (often unimportant) aspect of a complex stimulus, and to ignore other relevant aspects. This can make many DISCRIMINATIONS difficult or impossible (e.g., imagine trying to select a $1 or $5 bill, selecting by shape or size but not denomination). This is an example of selective STIMULUS CONTROL. Also see RELEVANT FEATURES OF STIMULI.

OVERT BEHAVIOR: Within the RADICAL BEHAVIORISM paradigm, a term used for behavior that can be observed by more than one individual. If I lift my soda can, this is an example of overt behavior, it is observable by anyone watching. In contrast, if I were to think about lifting my soda can, that would be COVERT BEHAVIOR (observable only to the individual engaging in the behavior). It is important to note that radical behaviorists do not regard COVERT BEHAVIOR as any less lawful or determined than more overt behavior. So there. (Sorry, we probably should have *thought about* that last comment.)

PAIRING: In the CLASSICAL CONDITIONING paradigm, a procedure whereby UNCONDITIONED and CONDITIONED stimuli are presented together. Within the operant paradigm, the procedure whereby a previously neutral stimulus becomes a reinforcer through being presented along with more naturally reinforcing stimuli. See SECONDARY, CONDITIONED, and GENERALIZED REINFORCERS, TOKEN ECONOMY. (It also refers to what we were forced to do at grade school dance recitals.)

PARALLEL PLAY: This is a term that refers to two individuals engaging in the same type of play simultaneously, but not necessarily interacting or even taking notice of one another.

PARTIAL INTERVAL RECORDING: A DATA SAMPLING procedure wherein time is broken up into specific intervals, and the observer records whether or not a target behavior occurred at least once during a given interval. A percentage measure of the number of intervals wherein the behavior was observed is derived. This type of data collection can provide a good estimation of the incidence of a given behavior, but may also slightly over-estimate incidence of behavior.

P.E.C.S.: Acronym used to refer to the Picture Exchange Communication System, a popular form of AUGMENTATIVE COMMUNICATION. See the work of Pyramid Educational Consultants.

PERCENT CORRECT: A behavioral measure in which data are expressed in terms of a given number of correct responses out of all responses. For example, a student might get 7 out of 10 responses correct, for a 70% score. Often maligned, this can be a very useful estimate of performance, as long as one looks at specific patterns within the data. This is often used to indicate MASTERY CRITERION on a task.

PERCEPTION: What a person "makes of" a particular stimulus; in everyday usage the way that sensations are understood and organized. Contrast with SENSATION. Individuals may perceive the same stimulus in markedly different ways, hence the need for INTER-OBSERVER AGREEMENT. A person's pre-existing biases may lead him/her to interpret events in unusual ways. To illustrate this, note the different ways people may understand the same physical stimulus (such as a song lyric). For example, we concluded the TOILET TRAINING section with a joke that features a commonly misinterpreted song lyric ("bad moon on the rise" becomes "bathroom on the right"). Note some other famous and common misinterpretations, and see if you've been guilty:

A. "Life could be ecstacy, you and me endlessly" becomes "...you and me and Leslie."

B. "Precious and few are the moments we two can share" becomes "...are the moments we toucans share."

C. "The girl with kaleidoscope eyes" becomes "the girl with colitis goes by."

D. "Excuse me while I kiss the sky" becomes "...while I kiss this guy." It's all in good fun while we're discussing song lyrics, but becomes much more serious when we start discussing functions of behavior. Often, inappropriate behavior is misinterpreted as someone willfully "being bad," when in fact they may actually simply be demonstrating a skill deficit.

PERFORMANCE: This term refers to what an individual actually does. It is sometimes used to contrast with ABILITY, which is used in everyday conversation to refer to what a person is capable of doing. Performance and ability may differ, depending on motivation and a myriad of other factors. What other factors? Everything you've been reading about up to now, and hopefully everything after!

PERSEVERATION: To engage in a behavior repeatedly. This behavior can be verbal (e.g., repeating phrases over and over) or nonverbal (e.g., watching the same 10 seconds of video tape over and over, or engaging in repetitive body movements). This term is often used to refer to behavior that was once classified as SELF-STIMULATORY. Perseveration is a preferred term because it does not suggest a FUNCTION for the behavior.

PERSON-CENTERED PLANNING: This term refers to an approach to program and placement construction wherein the student is an active participant in designing the program. His/her wants, needs, and interests are given the strongest weight in planning.

PERSONALIZED SYSTEM OF INSTRUCTION: This term is sometimes abbreviated PSI, and fondly referred to as the "Keller Method" in honor of FRED S. KELLER. PSI emphasizes students working independently and moving at their own pace through material, achieving MASTERY CRITERION of one MODULE before moving on to the next, the use of teachers as "coaches" or as supplements rather than as the primary source of teachings, and constant feedback (often written) back and forth between teacher and student. To use this method effectively, carefully constructed and empirically-verified MODULES must be created prior to attempts to teach.

PIVOTAL RESPONSE TRAINING: Refers to a general approach to teaching that emphasizes certain responses considered crucial to an individual's development. The responses that are chosen tend to be those that bring the individual into contact with a great deal of other social behavior and reinforcement. The ability to greet or share, for example, might be considered pivotal responses, in that they bring the individual into contact with potent sources of social reinforcement. See the work of Robert and Lynn Koegel and colleagues.

POSITION BIAS: This refers to the tendency of a student to choose items based upon their position in an array. A student with a "right bias" will generally choose the item placed on his right in a RECEPTIVE drill. This is often the result of teaching where the INTERVENTIONIST has not been careful to make sure that the correct item varies in position, and is an example of selective STIMULUS CONTROL. Also see LOOSE TEACHING and MATCHING TO SAMPLE.

POSITIVE: In technical "behaviorspeak," refers to the presentation of a stimulus, as in POSITIVE REINFORCEMENT and POSITIVE PUNISHMENT. The key is that the term is not a value judgement, but rather a description of a behavior –> consequence relationship (e.g., if you do a favor for another individual and they give you thanks or a gift). Contrast with NEGATIVE.

POSITIVE BEHAVIORAL SUPPORT: A term that refers to an

approach to human behavior that most individuals within ABA describe simply as another term for ABA. Some adherents, however, suggest that Positive Behavioral Support is something different. Those who see a difference suggest that Positive Behavioral Support includes (above and beyond the other aspects of applied behavior analytic thinking) a strict prohibition on AVERSIVES, and emphasizes social justice considerations and systems-level change. See an excellent review by Carr and Sidener (2002).

POSITIVE PRACTICE: This procedure is a sub-type of OVERCORRECTION. With this procedure, the individual repeatedly practices an appropriate behavior, contingent on having not performed the behavior at the appropriate time, or upon having performed an inappropriate version of the behavior (e.g., requiring appropriate walking in the hallway after inappropriately running down the hall).

POSITIVE PUNISHMENT: A CONTINGENCY in which the presentation of a particular stimulus following a given target behavior leads to a decrease in the future probability of that target behavior. As with other consequences, it is important to remember that a stimulus is only a POSITIVE PUNISHER if its contingent presentation leads to a decrease in the future probability of the target behavior. For example, if a parent scolds a child following a given inappropriate behavior, and the behavior <u>increases</u> in future probability, we cannot call that punishment. See also PUNISHMENT.

POSITIVE REINFORCEMENT: A CONTINGENCY wherein a particular stimulus is presented following a given target behavior, and this leads to an increase in the future probability of that target behavior. As with other consequences, it is important to remember that a stimulus is only a POSITIVE REINFORCER if its contingent presentation leads to an increase in the future probability of the behavior. Consider praise. Some students have not yet learned to find praise reinforcing, and its delivery has no behavior-altering effects. Some students find praise reinforcing only if it is quiet and casual. Other find it most reinforcing when presented with some enthusiasm ("EVERYTHING LOUDER THAN EVERYTHING ELSE," as Jim Steinman and Meat Loaf would say). See also REINFORCEMENT. Not to be confused with UNCONDITIONAL POSITIVE REGARD.

POST-REINFORCEMENT PAUSE: This refers to a period of relative inactivity after receipt of a reinforcer. This is generally most pronounced in FIXED RATIO schedules of reinforcement, particularly when there is a comparatively lean schedule (i.e., a large number of responses are needed in order to obtain reinforcement). Easily observed in college students when final exams are completed!

PRECISION TEACHING: A subset of ABA teaching methodology. In precision teaching, instructional methodology is based upon precisely targeted and often continuously self-monitored behavior, generally with the use of a STANDARD CELERATION CHART.

PREDICTION AND CONTROL: The criteria of understanding popularized by B.F. SKINNER. We understand a behavior when we can predict when it will occur. This prediction is based upon a full knowledge of the ANTECEDENT and CONSEQUENCE variables controlling the given behavior. If we can control those variables, we should also be able to make the behavior in question more or less likely. Also see CONTROL.

PREMACK REINFORCER: Access to a high probability behavior is used to reinforce a lower probability behavior. This is sometimes also called "Grandma's rule." This describes a straight-forward CONTINGENCY wherein access to a highly desired activity (e.g., going out to play) is made contingent upon the completion of a less desired activity (e.g., doing homework). As always when discussing reinforcement, the contingent delivery of the stimulus must lead to an increase in the future probability of the behavior to be properly called a reinforcer. See ACTIVITY REINFORCER.

PRIMARY REINFORCER: A reinforcer that is effective without any prior learning (i.e., is in-born). Even though these are often biologically-based stimuli, they need not be.

PRIVATE EVENTS: In the RADICAL BEHAVIORISM philosophy, refers to behavior that is not accessible to another individual. This is often used to refer to internal states such as thoughts and feelings. An important aspect of radical behavioral theory is that these events are not considered any less lawful nor determined than more public behavior. See also COVERT BEHAVIOR and OVERT BEHAVIOR.

PROBE: The name given to the procedure of "testing" programs. An example of a probe trial might involve introducing a step into motor imitation drills that has never been taught before, to assess if GENERALIZATION has occurred. This is sometimes also used in discussions of conducting BASELINES to determine functioning levels and appropriate programming. The term is also sometimes used to refer to data that is collected only for a student's first response to a particular stimulus.

PROMPT: An added antecedent stimulus that brings about a specific behavior. For example, if a child encounters a peer in the hallway but doesn't say "hi," a teacher may mouth the word "hi" or wave her hand. In this case, the prompts provided by the teacher make the desired behavior more likely. (Think of prompts as "hints"). Eventually, these prompts must be FADED so that the DISCRIMINATIVE STIMULUS (encountering the peer in the hallway) leads to the appropriate behavior. It should be noted that the term, PROMPT, is sometimes used in different ways. Some insist on a technical definition that includes that the prompt is successful in getting the behavior to occur (e.g., a hand-over-hand prompt that guides the individual through a behavior). Others use this term more loosely, referring to any antecedent stimulus, regardless of behavioral effect (e.g., "I delivered a verbal prompt, but he didn't respond."). Prompts can be provided across any sensory modality (e.g., visual prompts, verbal prompts, physical prompts, etc.). See also FADING,

PROMPT FADING and PROMPT DEPENDENCY. It should be noted that there is a particular set of techniques within speech therapy that is collectively referred to as P.R.O.M.P.T. This is an acronym, and not what is generally referred to in "behaviorspeak" when people refer to prompts or prompting.

PROMPT DEPENDENCY: Brought about by poor teaching, this refers to a condition wherein individuals do not respond to a DISCRIMINATIVE STIMULUS unless they receive prompts beyond what typically developing individuals require in order to respond. An example might be a student with developmental delays who waits to receive a physical prompt before he complies with a verbal instruction (DISCRIMINATIVE STIMULUS). Prompt dependency is generally created through poor execution of PROMPT FADING procedures.

PROMPT FADING: The procedure of gradually and systematically reducing extra stimuli that have been introduced by the INTERVENTIONIST to help in the teaching situation. It should be noted that failure to do this properly may lead to PROMPT DEPENDENCY.

PRO-SOCIAL BEHAVIOR: Behavior that benefits or assists another. Examples include helping someone who is hurt or assisting someone with a difficult task. Acquiring such skills often promotes productive social interactions.

PSYCHOTROPIC MEDICATION: Medications whose primary purpose is to affect behavioral or psychological functioning.

PUBLIC POSTING: This term refers to a STAFF TRAINING and FEEDBACK procedure wherein performance goals are displayed in such a way that everyone can see them. For example, the number of MANDS a student EMITS each day, or the number of training MODULES completed by a staff member, might be kept on a GRAPH on a bulletin board. More informally, remember your parents taping your good report cards to the fridge?

PUNISHMENT: The CONTINGENCY between a specific behavior and its consequence that will lead to a decrease in the future probability of the target behavior.   Also see POSITIVE and NEGATIVE PUNISHMENT.   Absolutely not to confused with NEGATIVE REINFORCEMENT, or else!

PUNISHER: A stimulus whose contingent presentation leads to a decrease in the future probability of the behavior that preceded it. As with REINFORCERS, it is important to note that PUNISHERS are defined in terms of their effect on future behavior. A stimulus is only a PUNISHER if delivering it following a particular behavior leads to a decrease in the future probability of that behavior (e.g., if a verbal reprimand following a child's running out into traffic leads to lessened running into traffic in the future). It should be noted that the same stimulus (e.g., a particular type of music) may serve as a reinforcer for one student, but function as a PUNISHER for another student.   That explains why certain individuals are "a little bit country," while others are a "little bit rock and roll."   See also AVERSIVES.

PYRAMIDAL TRAINING APPROACH: This is a term referring to a particular style of staff training and supervision. On top ("at the peak") of the pyramid is a single person who is meant to be the overall expert. This person supervises/trains a very small number of people, each of whom supervises/trains a slightly larger number, etc., down to the large "base" of staff who are being supervised by the comparatively fewer, more highly trained and experienced staff (e.g., see Page, Iwata, & Reid, 1982).

RADICAL BEHAVIORISM: The philosophy of BEHAVIORISM associated with B. F. SKINNER. On the crucial topic of PRIVATE EVENTS/COVERT BEHAVIOR, Skinner believed that these could be an area of proper study and were not less determined than more public behavior. This doesn't seem so radical to us!

RANDOMIZATION: A term used in DISCRETE TRIAL TEACHING, this refers to steps that have been MASTERED when presented on their own (in ISOLATION) that are now being practiced intermingled with other items. A person might begin with a BLOCK OF TRIALS that included only black and white in color identification, or perhaps only black alone.   When labels for many colors have been mastered, however, a single randomized block might include black, white, blue, red, green, brown, purple, pink, orange, and yellow. In programming, it is common to have one or two steps being worked on in isolation, and another set of steps being worked on randomly.

RANDOM ASSIGNMENT: When doing a BETWEEN GROUPS EXPERIMENT, subjects are assigned into groups on a non-systematic basis. The two characteristics of a random SAMPLE are:

1. Each person has an equal chance of being chosen for the experimental or control group.

2. Each sample is equally as likely as every other sample. Random assignment is used to attempt to CONTROL for subject variables within a given experiment.

RANGE: This term is used when discussing behavioral VARIABILITY. It refers to the difference between the highest and lowest values of a given DEPENDENT VARIABLE. For example, a child emitted between 3 and 10 social initiations on each day observed. Contrast with MEAN.

RATE: A measure of frequency across a specific period of time. For example, a child emits seven initiations per hour.

RATIO RUN: A term most often used to describe behavior under FIXED RATIO schedules of reinforcement. Following the POST-REINFORCEMENT PAUSE, the individual engages in very rapid responding. This rapid rate of responding stops when the individual obtains the reinforcer. To see a great example, watch a child shovel down spinach so she can get the dessert.

REACTIVITY: Often used in connection with SELF-MONITORING, this term refers to behavioral changes that occur simply because the behavior is being measured by the person (e.g., decreasing the total number of cigarettes smoked once one begins to record smoking).

REASONABLE ATTEMPTS: This is a term that refers to a general teaching approach wherein a behavior need not be as precise as prior PERFORMANCE in order to qualify for reinforcement. As long as the RESPONSE falls within the general class of correct responses, it would be reinforced, even if better examples of the behavior had been EMITTED previously. Also see APPROXIMATION.

RECEPTIVE PROGRAMS: Term used to refer to teaching programs that call on the student to follow an instruction. An example might be a "receptive color identification" program where the student is shown two colored objects and asked to identify the specified color by touching it.

RECOVERY: This is a term that is used when a student had previously been diagnosed with an autistic-spectrum disorder, but now shows no signs of the former diagnosis.

REDIRECTION: This term refers to a procedure wherein one individual attempts to interrupt a student engaging in a behavior (often an inappropriate behavior) and attempts to engage him/her in an alternate (generally more appropriate) behavior. Well known to parents whose children seem to prefer the other side of the street.

REIFICATION: This term refers to treating hypothetical concepts as though they were real, concrete items. Sometimes this is referred to as taking an adjective and turning it into a noun. Early psychodynamic theorists, for example, talked of nonconscious processes. They used the term as an adjective, simply referring to processing that was outside awareness. Later theorists talked of THE unconscious, as though it were a specific place. Other common terms in psychology such as personality and intelligence also suffer from some degree of reification. Now where did I leave that superego?

REINFORCEMENT: The contingency between a specific behavior and its consequence that leads to a future increase in the probability of the target behavior. Contrast with PUNISHMENT. Also see POSITIVE and NEGATIVE REINFORCEMENT, REINFORCER.

REINFORCER: A consequence that increases the future probability of the behavior that immediately preceded it. In other words, if you engage in a behavior, and that act produces a reinforcing outcome, then you are more likely to perform that behavior in the future. A simple example would be asking directions. You engage in the behavior of asking for directions, and receive the reinforcing outcome of being told how to reach your destination. It is important to note that all consequences are *not* reinforcers. A consequence is only a reinforcer if its contingent presentation leads to a future increase in the probability of the behavior that preceded the consequence. If you deliver a consequence and it does not lead to an increase in the future probability of the behavior that preceded the consequence, then that consequence is *not* a reinforcer. It might be neutral (no effect), or it might even be a PUNISHER (decrease in future probability of behavior). It should also be noted that reinforcement has nothing to do with what you intend when you deliver a given consequence, and that we sometimes *accidentally* reinforce behavior (see, for example, the examples listed in the section on NEGATIVE REINFORCEMENT). A great deal of the actual activity of behavior analysis entails discovering what reinforcers may inadvertently be maintaining behavior. As a final note, it is important that reinforcers be defined solely in terms of their effect on behavior (increasing the probability of that particular behavior). It is better not to speak of an individual "liking" the consequence, as this can lead us onto the wrong track. If an individual is more likely to engage in a particular behavior (e.g., throwing items) if throwing leads to his being yelled at, then being yelled at is still a reinforcer. He may not "like" being yelled at, but it is functioning as a reinforcer.

REINFORCER ASSESSMENT: One of the hallmarks of INDIVIDUALIZATION in ABA, this is a procedure to identify the stimuli and activities that a student finds reinforcing. This can be accomplished by simply leaving an individual alone with stimuli and activities, and seeing what the student gravitates towards. It can also be accomplished by presenting stimuli in pairs, and constructing a hierarchy based upon which are chosen by the student from the pairs. If doing this choice procedure, make sure to present items several times, with each stimulus/activity paired with many different items/activities. It is important to note that reinforcer assessments should be conducted frequently, as reinforcer effectiveness may change rapidly due to DEPRIVATION and SATIATION effects.

RELATED SERVICES: This term refers to a variety of therapies that are commonly offered in school programs (e.g., speech therapy, occupational therapy, physical therapy, counseling, etc.). It should be noted that many ABA programs reason that "behavior is behavior" and do not use related service providers. Another common strategy is to use related service providers, but to have all these providers use the same ABA-based teaching methodologies (e.g., a speech therapist teaching via a specified DISCRETE TRIAL TEACHING or NATURAL ENVIRONMENTAL TEACHING approach, or an occupational therapist using a SHAPING and CHAINING methodology to teach zippering skills). A general ABA bias is that "everyone does everything." In keeping with the frequently observed FAILURE TO GENERALIZE, it is generally not good practice to have specific skills being worked on only by specific individuals. If a related service provider designs a specific program based upon his/her evaluations, the next step is to teach everyone else involved in programming how to implement the teaching. It is a tenet of ABA that under no circumstances should anyone (related service providers included) employ techniques that have not been EMPIRICALLY VERIFIED as effective. See Needelman (2000) for further background.

RELEVANT (CRITICAL) FEATURES OF STIMULI: Refers to the specific characteristics of a stimulus or situation that occasion a particular behavior. For example, if a child correctly points to a red square when instructed to do so, but does not point to a blue one, we can infer that the relevant feature of the stimulus in this case is the color red. See also DISCRIMINATION, DISCRIMINATIVE STIMULUS, STIMULUS OVERSELECTIVITY, and GENERALIZATION.

RESISTANCE TO EXTINCTION: A measure of the amount of responding emitted by a given individual following cessation of reinforcement. Generally speaking, INTERMITTENT SCHEDULES OF REINFORCEMENT lead to greater resistance to extinction than CONTINUOUS REINFORCEMENT schedules. See EXTINCTION.

RESPONDENT CONDITIONING: See CLASSICAL CONDITIONING.

RESPONSE: This is a term that is often used synonymously with BEHAVIOR, but generally refers to a behavior in reaction to a particular stimulus.

RESPONSE CLASS: A group of responses that serve the same function, even if different in TOPOGRAPHY. One might turn off a light, for example, with a flick of a finger, or the palm of the hand, or by leaning on it, or with a well-placed axe kick (as demonstrated one particularly memorable night in graduate school by Dr. Nancy Hemmes, one of the best professors of ABA of all time). The response class of "instruction-following," for example, would refer to the general act of following verbal directions. See GENERALIZATION.

RESPONSE COST: A NEGATIVE PUNISHMENT procedure wherein an individual loses a previously earned reinforcer, contingent upon inappropriate behavior. Some clinicians feel that this may not always be a good idea, as it can cut down on the value of reinforcers (i.e., why should I work hard to obtain a reinforcer if it can just be taken from me anyway?). This notwithstanding, Ken Reeve wishes it to be known that this is how his mother taught him to stop using "gutter talk."

REVERSAL DESIGN: Along with MULTIPLE BASELINE, one of the basic SINGLE-SUBJECT research designs. With a reversal design, an individual is exposed to "condition A" (say, a BASELINE). Once STABILITY in behavior is achieved, the individual is exposed to "condition B" (a given treatment). Once the effect of condition B is ascertained and stability is achieved, condition A would be reinstated. Reversals can be repeated several times, and several conditions may be implemented. The basic logic of the reversal design rests in the ability of the experimenter to measure behavioral effects as treatments are implemented and then withdrawn. It provides EMPIRICALLY VERIFIED results of treatment procedures. See also INTERNAL VALIDITY.

RFFC: RECEPTIVE categorization according to the Function, Feature, or Class of an object. Examples of:

Function: "what do we eat with?"

Feature: "which one bounces?"

Class: "which one is a toy?"

See also CATEGORY, STIMULUS CLASS, EXEMPLARS, RELEVANT

FEATURES OF STIMULI.

RIGHT TO EFFECTIVE BEHAVIORAL TREATMENT: This is an ethical stance adopted by behavior analysts. It holds that individuals with disabilities have the right to expect that treatments that have been EMPIRICALLY VERIFIED as effective will be implemented on their behalf. It also holds that treatments that have not been EMPIRICALLY VERIFIED as effective should not be implemented, until such time as they can be demonstrated to be effective in properly CONTROLLED research (see EXPERIMENT). Individuals also have the right to programs that teach skills that will help them to lead more independent lives, to have their own welfare be a primary goal of intervention, to treatment by competent behavior analysts, and to on-going behavioral assessment and evaluation. Individuals have a right to the most effective treatment available, in keeping with the LEAST RESTRICTIVE TREATMENT model. If necessary, individuals have a right to expect more intrusive procedures that will be effective in ameliorating their difficulties, in contrast to less intrusive procedures that are not shown to be effective.

ROMANCZYK, RAYMOND G.: The best lecturer on the planet.

RULE-GOVERNED BEHAVIOR: Behavior that is under the control of verbal (spoken or written) descriptions of behavior –> consequence relationships. The individual need not have actually experienced the CONTINGENCY, only the verbal description of the behavior –>

consequence relationship. For example, if a student is told that if he studies hard he will make a lot of money later, and he does in fact study harder, that would be an example of rule-governed behavior. Some people use this term to distinguish such behavior from CONTINGENCY-SHAPED BEHAVIOR. In the latter, the individual has actually experienced the consequences. See also INSENSITIVITY TO REINFORCEMENT.

S^D: Pronounced "Ess Dee," this is the symbolic notation for DISCRIMINATIVE STIMULUS. This is a stimulus that signals that a given behavior will be reinforced. In teaching programs, it is crucial to vary verbal PROMPTS so that a student does not become dependent on a particular phrasing (e.g., "touch" versus "show me" or "give me" or "which one is" or "point to," etc.). See also EXEMPLAR, DISCRIMINATION, GENERALIZATION, STIMULUS CONTROL.

S DELTA: Represented by an S with a super-scripted triangle, this is the symbolic notation for a stimulus that signals that a given behavior will either not be reinforced or may be punished. Most of us remember that face our Dads made that signaled to us, "If you clown around just once more...."

S^{R+}: The symbolic notation for POSITIVE REINFORCEMENT.

SALIENCE: This term refers to how important or noticeable a given stimulus is within the environment. May also refer to a component of a stimulus (see RELEVANT FEATURES).

SAMPLE: A small part of a larger population that is chosen to participate in an experiment. Also what you do to the food at a large buffet.

SATIATION: When a reinforcer loses its effectiveness through overuse. PRIMARY REINFORCERS are particularly susceptible to this effect. When you have eaten too much, you may be "full" and not want any more food reinforcers. This can also occur with ACTIVITY (PREMACK) reinforcers, with the individual "getting tired" of an activity. GENERALIZED REINFORCERS tend to be most immune to satiation. How many people do you know who get tired of getting money? This term is also used to refer to a behavior management strategy in which an individual receives a given reinforcer noncontingently, in the attempt to break a relationship between some inappropriate behavior and the reinforcer. See also ESTABLISHING OPERATION.

SCALLOPING: A pattern of responding associated with FIXED INTERVAL schedules of reinforcement. This pattern is characterized by a relative lack of responding following reinforcement, a rate which accelerates as the time of reinforcement approaches (e.g., waiting until the second week in April to begin working on income taxes, or waiting until the night before an exam to begin studying). Not to be confused with anything having to do with mollusks or what a horse does when it runs quickly.

SCHEDULE OF REINFORCEMENT: A statement of the ratio of responses to reinforcers.   This can be CONTINUOUS or INTERMITTENT. If INTERMITTENT, the schedule can be FIXED or VARIABLE.   It should be noted that some people also refer to EXTINCTION as a schedule of reinforcement.

SCHEDULING: This term refers to emitting a behavior at a specified time, noncontingently. In breaking nicotine addiction, for example, a person might smoke on a schedule rather than when having nicotine cravings, thereby breaking the NEGATIVE REINFORCEMENT relationship smoking has with "nicotine fits" (smoking decreases the "fits"). When a behavior is determined to have a sensory FUNCTION, sometimes the individual is allowed access to the stimulus/activity on a schedule, rather than in response to a specific behavior.

SCIENCE: A process of learning ("knowing") about how events in the world operate, based on first-hand observation of these events in action (see EMPIRICALLY VERIFIED). In basic and applied behavior analysis, the question generally concerns how specific events in a person's environment affect specific behavior of that individual. These observations are first worded as specific predictions (hypotheses) that are later tested to see whether they are supported. Such observations are made under controlled conditions that allow the investigator to rule out ("CONTROL") the effects of other events (see also EXPERIMENT). For example, if a prediction is made that observing a video model will increase the likelihood that a child will engage in a particular play activity, this can be tested by presenting the video model while not presenting any other instructional procedures for that task. We can then record any increases in the play activity as a result of the presentation of the video model. Also see SCIENTIFIC METHOD and FALSIFIABLE.

SCIENTIFIC METHOD: This term refers to a group of procedures for making data-based decisions. It has several key components. It is cumulative, in that it builds upon prior gathered knowledge. Its findings are EMPIRICAL, and based upon careful observation and CONTROLLED research. It avoids TAUTOLOGIES. It avoids REIFICATION. Its findings are FALSIFIABLE. It is apolitical. Its findings are subject to replication. Also see SCIENCE.

SCRIPTING: This term refers to a general approach to planning in some key areas (e.g., language, play, etc.). The person is led through a pre-established set of steps (verbal and/or nonverbal) to practice a given skill. This may take the form of a scripted conversation or SYMBOLIC PLAY or some other similar sort of activity. A key component is to teach people to follow scripts in general, and not just to learn one particular script. This should facilitate GENERALIZATION.

SECONDARY REINFORCER: A CONSEQUENCE that was previously NEUTRAL, but has become a reinforcer through PAIRING with a previously established reinforcer. Money becomes a secondary reinforcer by being paired with the commodities it purchases. Interventionists may become secondary reinforcers through being paired with other reinforcers (e.g., praise, tokens, favored activities, etc.).   Also called a CONDITIONED REINFORCER.   Also see GENERALIZED REINFORCER.

SELECTION BIAS: This term refers to an experimental result that only happens because a special SAMPLE of subjects was used. For example, if we assess the effects of a RECEPTIVE color identification program, but select children who are color blind, it would appear that the teaching program "was not effective."

SELECTIONISM: A term used by some to refer to the behavioral approach. The consequences of behavior "select" which responses will be "kept" (made again) by the individual and which will be lost. In this way, it is similar to the evolutionary natural selection process discussed by Darwin and later scientists regarding biological variations.   Also   see   SHAPING   and   DIFFERENTIAL REINFORCEMENT.

SELF-CONTROL: The opposite of IMPULSIVITY. Refers to the tendency to engage in a behavior that produces a more delayed (but larger) reward as opposed to engaging in a behavior that will produce a more immediate (but smaller) reward. Students who are studying now in order to acquire a good grade on the exam in two weeks, as opposed to going out to have a good time now, are demonstrating SELF-CONTROL.

SELF-HELP SKILLS: See ACTIVITIES OF DAILY LIVING.

SELF-INJURY (SELF-INJURIOUS BEHAVIOR, SIB): The act of causing physical injury to one's self. The most common forms are hitting one's head or body with a hand, banging of the head into objects such as a table or wall, and biting of one's own hand. It must be emphasized that there may be a variety of functions maintaining this behavior. Therefore, a careful FUNCTIONAL ANALYSIS must be conducted to ensure proper BEHAVIOR TREATMENT PLAN creation to eliminate the self-injurious behavior.

SELF-INSTRUCTIONAL TRAINING: A procedure wherein an individual is taught to talk him/herself through a particular activity. The person at first talks out loud, describing the current step and next required step as (s)he performs the BEHAVIOR CHAIN. Eventually, this overt vocalizing becomes covert. See the work of Donald Meichenbaum.

SELF-MANAGEMENT: A term that refers to the procedures of self-monitoring and self-reinforcement. People self-manage when they observe their own behavior and self-deliver reinforcers based upon meeting behavioral criteria. Also used as a synonym for SELF-CONTROL in traditional educational settings.

SELF-MONITORING: The act of measuring one's own behavior. In the clinical literature, this has sometimes been reported to affect behavior in and of itself (a phenomenon known as REACTIVITY). For example, reduced smoking may occur as one counts the number of cigarettes one smokes in a given day.

SELF-REINFORCEMENT: The self-delivery of consequences, leading to an increase in the future probability of the behavior that preceded REINFORCEMENT. As with other forms of reinforcement, this term is reserved for when the CONTINGENT delivery of the CONSEQUENCE leads to an increase in the future probability of the target behavior, and not just for the act of self-delivering a consequence. It must be remembered that not all consequences are reinforcers. Some stimuli are neutral, some might even function as punishers.

SELF-STIMULATORY BEHAVIOR: Sometimes inappropriately referred to as "stimming" as a shorthand, this is a term that refers to behavior whose presumed FUNCTION is to provide some sort of sensory feedback. This term should be used sparingly, as it can be a TAUTOLOGY and therefore quite misleading. Calling a behavior "self-stimulatory" might lead one to believe that the behavior is occurring for simple sensory feedback, when in fact there may be a very different function. Much "self-stimulatory" behavior actually serves an ATTENTION-SEEKING, AVOIDANCE, or COMMUNICATION function. As with all other areas within ABA, a FUNCTIONAL ANALYSIS must be conducted before the behavior can be understood. Also referred to as STEREOTYPIC BEHAVIOR.

SELF-TALK: This term refers to speaking, but these utterances are not meant for other individuals to hear. Such behavior can be socially appropriate or inappropriate. This can take the form of verbal PERSEVERATION (probably socially inappropriate), or may serve as a rehearsal for behavior the individual will engage in (possibly socially appropriate).   Also see SELF-INSTRUCTIONAL TRAINING.

SEND LAWYERS, GUNS AND MONEY: Slang expression taken from Warren Zevon song of the same name. Generally used in response to the question, "how was your day?" It basically indicates a day from hell.

SENSATION: The physical experiencing of a particular stimulus. Contrast with PERCEPTION.

SENSITIZATION: This term refers to an individual having a greater reaction to a particular stimulus after repeated exposure to the stimulus.   In everyday language, considered the opposite of HABITUATION.

SESAME STREET/THE MUPPETS: The apex of contributions to civilization.

SETTING EVENT: A stimulus-response interaction that will affect stimulus-response interactions that occur later. If a student has been teased by classmates before class, for example, this may alter his behavior when he enters the classroom setting. While there is a technical difference, used interchangeably by some people with ESTABLISHING OPERATION.

SHAPING: A very powerful process used to create new behavior by differentially reinforcing successive APPROXIMATIONS to a desired behavior (the target response). To successfully shape behavior, one must:

A. Begin by reinforcing a crude approximation to the target response.

B. After a time, put that crude approximation on EXTINCTION (i.e., do not reinforce the crude approximation again).

C. An EXTINCTION BURST will set in, which will lead to a greater frequency and magnitude of behavior, as well as variability in the behavior.

D. As a result of the variability seen with the extinction burst, a closer approximation to the target behavior may be performed.

E. Reinforce this closer approximation.

F. Repeat steps A-E until the target response is emitted perfectly.

As an analogy, think of the children's game, "Hot and Cold."

SHARING EXPERIENCES: This term refers to one individual attempting to point out something of interest in the environment to another individual. This is an extremely important social behavior that is often the target of teaching in behavioral programming. See also JOINT ATTENTION.

SHORT-DELAY CONDITIONING: In CLASSICAL CONDITIONING, this is a pairing procedure wherein the CONDITIONED STIMULUS precedes the UNCONDITIONED STIMULUS by a short interval (often less than two seconds) and slightly overlaps with it. This is generally the most effective form of CLASSICAL CONDITIONING pairing. For example, a child quickly learns the value of a TOKEN when it is paired with an already established REINFORCER in this manner.

SIGN LANGUAGE: This term refers to a highly developed system of AUGMENTATIVE COMMUNICATION. Hand gestures refer to specific concepts and letters of the alphabet, and are combined so as to allow an individual who cannot speak to communicate. There are numerous systems and "dialects" that are in use throughout the world.

SIGNAL RELATION: A term from the CLASSICAL CONDITIONING literature, this refers to the idea that a CONDITIONED STIMULUS will ELICIT a RESPONSE only if it provides information regarding the presentation of the UNCONDITIONED STIMULUS. Contrast with TEMPORAL CONTIGUITY. For golfers, think about why hearing "fore!" makes you drop to the ground.

SIMULTANEOUS CONDITIONING: In the CLASSICAL CONDITIONING paradigm, this entails presenting the UNCONDITIONED and CONDITIONED stimuli at precisely the same time. This does not tend to be as effective as SHORT-DELAY conditioning.

SINGLE-SUBJECT RESEARCH DESIGNS: These are experimental designs where each individual is the subject of analysis, and each subject serves as his/her own CONTROL. While the term is "single subject" design, there are often several individuals involved in each experiment. Each of five individuals might experience a particular REVERSAL or MULTIPLE BASELINE, for example. This is the most common form of EXPERIMENT presented in applied behavior analytic research, in keeping with the need for FUNCTIONAL ANALYSIS for treatments in question. See BETWEEN GROUPS DESIGN for contrast.

SKILL DEFICIT MODEL: This term refers to the general idea that much inappropriate behavior is a result of the individual not being able to perform other, more appropriate behavior. A person is being aggressive not as a form of noncompliance, for example, but rather because he does not know how to engage in more socially appropriate behavior. A student with autism may be avoiding eye contact not because it is aversive, but rather because she has not learned to screen out other distractions that draw her gaze.

SKINNER, B. F.: Scientist and philosopher whose writings form much of the background for ABA thinking and procedures. Suggested readings are included in the appendix. As it reads on a wonderful baseball cap given to me (BN) by the ELIJA Foundation, "B.F. SKINNER IS THE MAN."

SKINNERIAN CONDITIONING: Another term for OPERANT CONDITIONING, in tribute to B. F. Skinner, who did so much to elaborate and popularize the approach.

SLOPE: A term used in the analysis of graphs. This refers to the steepness of the gradient of the data line. Generally speaking, the steeper the slope, the more dramatic the behavior change. Also a favorite term of skiers as something to "hit."

SOCIAL REINFORCERS: Reinforcers that consist of interactions with other individuals.

SOCIAL SIGNIFICANCE: This is a concept referring to the degree to which a behavior change makes a difference in the life of the individual.   This is sometimes contrasted with STATISTICAL SIGNIFICANCE. A change in rate from 2,000 to 1,600 daily instances of SELF-INJURIOUS BEHAVIOR may be statistically significant, but would probably not be socially significant. See the definition of ABA.

SOCIAL VALIDITY: Most often used in terms of a comparison to typically developing peers. The rate of social initiations by typically developing students might be used to guide the goals of a social initiations program for a student demonstrating social difficulties.

STABILITY: A term used to refer to the degree of variability of a behavior under examination. Stability is generally sought during BASELINE, prior to the implementation of a given intervention. See also ASCENDING, DESCENDING, GRAPH, and VARIABILITY.

STAFF TRAINING: This is a general term for efforts to teach and practice skills with interventionists to help them to become more effective in carrying out teaching and behavior management programs. Also see PYRAMIDAL TRAINING APPROACH.

STANDARD CELERATION CHART: A type of graphing in use in many programs, a standard celeration chart is a semi-logarithmic, six cycle, chart that measures frequency of behavior per some unit of time.

STANDARDIZED TESTING: This term refers to a wide variety of assessment tools. They are called "standardized" in the sense that they have been administered to extremely large numbers of individuals so that typical performance across age levels and disabilities may be derived. An individual's scores are compared against this large pool of previous test takers. It should be noted when dealing with the autistic-spectrum disorders that many children are difficult or impossible to test with most common standardized measures. This may be due to an inability to follow directions, or to perform a specific skill (e.g., MATCHING TO SAMPLE or reading). This should not be interpreted to mean that a person with an autistic-spectrum disorder is somehow inherently MENTALLY RETARDED, but rather that specific skill deficits exist. "Guesstimate" is an insulting slang term used for test scores that are based upon testing that is inappropriate for a given student (e.g., a test in which the student cannot perform required skills, or a test that was standardized for different clinical or age groups). Tools exist to estimate functioning levels without actually testing the student (e.g., the VINELAND ADAPTIVE BEHAVIOR SCALES and CHILDHOOD AUTISM RATING SCALES, which involve observations and interviewing a caregiver regarding behavior observed and comparing this to age-standardized NORMS).

STATISTICAL SIGNIFICANCE: A concept that refers to the probability that a behavioral difference occurred due to chance and not as the result of a given intervention. This is frequently described in terms of a given numerical level of probability. Reaching a .01 level of significance indicates less than one chance in 100 that the observed difference is due to chance. A .05 level of significance indicates less than five chances in 100 that the observed difference is due to random factors, etc. This is not a term in common usage in ABA, but is used in more general educational and psychological research that relies on group experiments. Contrast with SOCIAL SIGNIFICANCE.

STATISTICS: These are often complex mathematical formulas used to ascertain the effects of given variables. Because of the emphasis on SOCIAL SIGNIFICANCE within ABA, these are not generally in wide usage within ABA.

STEREOTYPIC BEHAVIOR: See SELF-STIMULATORY BEHAVIOR.

STIMULUS CLASS: A set of stimuli (e.g., objects, people, situations) that occasion a common response. That is, we respond to all members of the set in a common way. For example, if a child can correctly point to all the girls in a room while ignoring the boys, those girls are serving as a stimulus class. Depending on the type of stimulus class, the members within a set may either resemble one another (such as a set of blocks that are all colored red) or they may not (such as the set made up of the written word CAT, the word cat spoken out loud, and a picture of a cat). In common language, people often refer to stimulus classes as "CATEGORIES." Also see EQUIVALENCE CLASS, DISCRIMINATIVE STIMULUS, GENERALIZATION.

STIMULUS CONTROL: A term that refers to behavioral control by antecedent conditions. Stimulus control is said to be demonstrated when behavior is EMITTED in the presence of one stimulus (THE DISCRIMINATIVE STIMULUS), but not in the presence of another stimulus (S DELTA). To see a great example, watch motorist behavior at an intersection with a traffic light. Stimulus control can also be demonstrated within a CLASSICAL CONDITIONING paradigm.

STIMULUS SUPERIMPOSITION: Used generally with students who might be described as OVERSELECTIVE, to help DISCRIMINATIONS to occur. For example, a student might be having difficulty learning the difference between a $1 bill and a $5 bill. They are both the same size, the same color, have portraits in the same place, have numbers in the same place, etc. The student is not able to recognize the few important differences that make the discrimination possible. A clinician might therefore alter the stimuli, by coloring in the "5's" in red, for example. With the addition of this superimposed stimulus, the student can now make the DISCRIMINATION. Of course, this superimposed stimulus must now be FADED back to normal conditions. Also see RELEVANT FEATURES OF STIMULI.

SUCCESSIVE APPROXIMATIONS: Within a shaping paradigm, the reinforced behavior steps as one creates a more exact version of the target behavior. See APPROXIMATION and SHAPING.

SUPERSTITION: This is most often associated with behavior learned through NONCONTINGENT REINFORCEMENT. An individual acts as though some specific response brings about reinforcement, when in fact the response in question is completely unrelated to the actual delivery of reinforcement. In college classes, you always get to see some wild hats worn during finals. Guess why!

SYMBOLIC PLAY: Refers to a type of play in which individuals use one object to represent another (e.g., a stick becomes an oar or a shirt becomes a wig). This can take the form of fairly elaborate play (e.g., when a frisbee becomes a steering wheel and the child takes everyone in the living room for a drive).

SYMPTOM SUBSTITUTION: The idea that if one eliminates one behavioral symptom without removing the "underlying" problem, then a new symptom will simply take the place of the eliminated symptom. This idea is generally held by those of a psychoanalytic orientation. The clinical literature does not support the reality of this concept, provided a proper FUNCTIONAL ANALYSIS has been conducted. If a proper FUNCTIONAL ANALYSIS has not been carried out, or if the concepts of a RESPONSE CLASS or EXTINCTION BURST are not properly appreciated, then something that looks like symptom substitution may occur. If one places avoidance-based SELF-INJURIOUS BEHAVIOR on EXTINCTION, for example, but does not place avoidance-based vomiting on extinction, it may appear that symptom substitution has taken place. In fact, all that has happened is that a behavioral variation associated with the EXTINCTION BURST has been reinforced.

SYSTEMATIC DESENSITIZATION: A technique often associated with introducing phobic or uncomfortable stimuli. The first step is to teach a student some sort of coping skill (e.g., deep relaxation). One would then construct a hierarchy of phobic or uncomfortable stimuli, going from least anxiety-provoking to most. For example, if someone were afraid of dogs, the first item on the hierarchy might be the written word "dog," the second item a photograph of a dog, the third item a video of a dog...up through the physical presence of actual dogs. The student would be helped to achieve his/her state of relaxation or other coping skill, and then the stimuli from the hierarchy would begin to be introduced, beginning with the least anxiety-provoking. In contrast to FLOODING, the desire is to minimize the student's experience of any sort of anxiety. As soon as a student shows any signs of discomfort, the anxiety-provoking stimulus would be removed and the relaxation restored. Only after relaxation has been achieved would the anxiety-provoking stimulus be reintroduced. When the student could experience an item from the hierarchy without discomfort, REINFORCEMENT would be delivered and the next item would be introduced. This would continue until the student could experience all items from the hierarchy without anxiety.

TACT: From Skinner's VERBAL BEHAVIOR, meaning "to label." This might entail labeling specific objects or occurrences. In programming, the final goal is generally spontaneous tacting, where the individual tacts without prompting (e.g., a child makes an initiation by describing an object to another child as a means of sharing experiences).

TANTRUM: A highly individualized RESPONSE CLASS referring to behavioral agitation following a specific stimulus. The response class often includes yelling or other loud voicing, crying, object destruction, and possibly aggression towards self or others. The functions of tantrums often include avoidance, frustration, or communication attempts. While not desirable to see, it should be noted that tantrums commonly occur as the individual learns to tolerate normalizing activities such as demand situations or typical levels of ambient noise. As Chris Rea reminded us in one of the lost hits of the 1970's (*Fool if you think it's over*), "Newborn eyes always cry with pain, first look at the morning Sun." Students should not be allowed to avoid normalizing activities through the use of tantrums, lest we accidentally NEGATIVELY REINFORCE the tantrum. Rather, the individual should be taught coping skills and gradually exposed to that which they find difficult.

TARGET BEHAVIOR: A response that we are making the object of analysis (e.g., to increase or decrease the probability of a given behavior). For example, programs often target "attending behavior" before other skills are taught.

TASK ANALYSIS: Used most often in discussions of CHAINING, this is a written list of all steps that must be accomplished to perform a particular behavior. It is most important to note that each task analysis must be individually constructed (see INDIVIDUALIZATION). Depending on the functioning level of an individual, a task analysis for a skill like setting a table might include ten steps, or might include 100 steps. The key is to begin teaching with a given task analysis, and to watch for where progress stops (the individual is not mastering the skill). The step at which progress has stopped must then be broken down into smaller steps. It is rare to begin teaching a skill with a given task analysis, and to finish with the same task analysis. They must constantly be rewritten, depending on student progress. The same task analysis will rarely be effective for two different individuals.

TAUTOLOGY: This refers to a circular definition. An example might be "selective mutism":

"Why isn't he speaking in school?"

"Because he has selective mutism!"

"How do you know he has selective mutism?"

"Well, he doesn't talk in school."

This should be avoided at all costs, as simply naming a phenomenon does not mean that we understand it. See also the flaw in the term

SELF-STIMULATORY BEHAVIOR.

TEACH ME LANGUAGE: Book by Freeman and Drake. It is in common usage for teaching conversational skills to individuals with developmental disabilities.

TEACHING STIMULI: This refers to the specific stimuli that are used in teaching programs. For generalization purposes, it is crucial to have several sets of stimuli for each concept one is attempting to teach (see EXEMPLAR). One cannot just teach with colored pieces of paper and expect that a student will spontaneously be able to label colors in crayons or other objects (see FAILURE TO GENERALIZE). Note: care must also be chosen so that stimuli vary only according to the dimension one is trying to teach (see RELEVANT FEATURES OF STIMULI). One would not use a wooden yardstick for "long," and a small red plastic ruler for "short." A student might choose correctly, but erroneously believe that "long" means "made of wood" or "brown," and "short" means "red" or "made of plastic."

TELEGRAPHIC PRAISE: A form of praise that describes the behavior. "Good sitting," "I like the way you're looking at me," "good passing the remote control, Dana" might be examples of telegraphic praise. This is also called BEHAVIOR-SPECIFIC PRAISE.

TEMPORAL CONTIGUITY: From the CLASSICAL CONDITIONING literature, this term refers to the idea that a NEUTRAL STIMULUS becomes a CONDITIONED STIMULUS simply by being paired in time with an UNCONDITIONED STIMULUS. This theory has not been supported in the EMPIRICAL literature. Contrast with SIGNAL RELATIONS.

THREE-TERM CONTINGENCY: Another expression for the A–> B –> C behavior-conceptualization system. Also see DISCRETE TRIAL TEACHING.

TIME-OUT FROM POSITIVE REINFORCEMENT: Called "time out" for short, this term refers to a collection of very often misused techniques. The general idea of time out is that a given reinforcer is removed for a short period of time, contingent upon some inappropriate behavior being EMITTED by an individual. While this can take the form of an individual having to go to a different setting (e.g., the common "time out" chair), time out need not take this form, and indeed there are good reasons to avoid this use (e.g., accidentally reinforcing with attention, or accidentally reinforcing AVOIDANCE behavior). Time out can be accomplished within the given setting (e.g., a television set is turned off for ten seconds following inappropriate arm flapping while watching). Also see RESPONSE COST and NEGATIVE PUNISHMENT.

TOILET TRAINING: This term refers to a set of procedures that teach an individual how to. . .Did we need to tell you this one? Seriously, as with LEISURE SKILLS, this is an important area to address. A lack of toileting skills can make people appear much lower-functioning than they actually are. Keeping in mind the DEAD

MAN'S TEST, it must be remembered that we are working on appropriate elimination, not just "holding it in." Intensive toilet training generally begins in the bathroom itself, with a great deal of time spent there attempting to encourage and REINFORCE appropriate elimination. See the work of Foxx and Azrin, etc. If you require any directions for how to get there, just remember Creedence Clearwater Revival: "There's a bathroom on the right."

TOKEN: An arbitrarily chosen stimulus that is serving as a GENERALIZED REINFORCER, often in a TOKEN ECONOMY. Common choices include coins, poker chips, stickers, pieces of puzzles or photographs. These are often used with velcro so as to allow for the creation of a "token board" on which they will be placed. Also see PAIRING, SECONDARY REINFORCER, CONDITIONED REINFORCER.

TOKEN ECONOMY: A system wherein individuals earn arbitrarily chosen stimuli, and these stimuli are used as GENERALIZED REINFORCERS as part of a behavior management or teaching system. The following is from *Graduated Applied Behavior Analysis* (reproduced with permission):

Setting up a token economy system is actually a great deal easier than many people suppose it to be. Briefly stated, token economies are a system of exchange whereby particular behavior earns tokens, and these tokens are then traded for other commodities. Token economies are particularly valuable as they are quite normalizing (we all get our paychecks that we trade in for other commodities) and stretch out the supply of other reinforcers (e.g., you may have to earn five tokens to trade it in for a primary). It is unlikely that a student will ever satiate using a generalized reinforcer system. There should always be something new to buy, always something new to get. Further, it is generally not necessary to employ deprivation procedures. Who do you know who thinks they have enough money? No matter how much you have, more is always nice. Contrast this with primary reinforcers such as food. With primaries, deprivation and satiation are serious issues.

To begin using the system, choose the commodity you are going to use. Poker chips, coins, stickers, decorated pieces of laminated cardboard, and points on a point board are common choices.

Once you have your commodity established, sit down with your student. Have a collection of the primary reinforcers (s)he has been earning ready to be used. Begin by simply giving the student the token noncontingently and immediately asking for it back and providing the primary reinforcer. Do this several times. Look for signs that the student is giving you the token without prompting and you know you are ready for the next step.

As you see that the student is now giving you the token back and anticipating the exchange, introduce a contingency. Ask the student to do something *you are certain (s)he can do easily.* Reinforce the performance of this behavior with the presentation of a token and immediately request it back to make the exchange just as you had when you were providing tokens noncontingently. This is your first contingently awarded token. Do this several times to establish the new system.

Of course, you really haven't gained anything yet. The student is still getting a primary reinforcer on every trial. Watch what you can do now, however. Ask the student to perform a skill you are certain (s)he can do, just as before. Award the token. When the student begins to trade in the token, however, quickly ask the student to perform the skill again. When the student does, award another token. Now the student will trade in *both tokens* for the primary. You are now on your way and can begin gradually building the student up to earning several tokens and trading them in. Make sure not to build up requirements too quickly or the behavior may extinguish. Gradually look for more and more accurate responses and longer intervals before trade-in. Keep the system potent, however, and build up patiently. Eventually, you will be able to have different systems working simultaneously (e.g., these pennies are for trading in for primaries for accurate responding during trials, while he also earns points on a board according to a DRO system aimed at reducing perseverative behavior. He'll trade in those points for a trip to the park at the end of the session, or the week, or whatever is appropriate for the student's functioning level).

TOPOGRAPHY: What a given behavior looks like. A description of the form of the behavior. Also see RESPONSE CLASS.

TOTAL TASK PRESENTATION: This term refers to a type of FORWARD CHAINING in which the individual is instructed in every single step of the TASK ANALYSIS during each session.

TRACE CONDITIONING: In the CLASSICAL CONDITIONING paradigm, a pairing arrangement such that the CONDITIONED STIMULUS is presented, is terminated, and then the UNCONDITIONED STIMULUS is presented. This is not generally effective in terms of teaching the individual to respond to the CONDITIONED STIMULUS, and may in fact have the opposite effect. In this pairing arrangement, the CONDITIONED STIMULUS signals that the UNCONDITIONED STIMULUS will *not* be coming. Only when the CONDITIONED STIMULUS ceases will the UNCONDITIONED STIMULUS appear.

TRANSITIONING: Switching from one activity to another. Many students with disabilities need specific treatment plans to help them learn to transition appropriately.

TRAVEL TRAINING: A set of procedures used to teach individuals with disabilities to get around independently, often through the use of public transportation systems.

TREND: This refers to behavior becoming more probable or less probable, often ascertained by examination of a GRAPH.

TWO FACTOR THEORY: This term refers to the use of a combination of CLASSICAL and OPERANT conditioning to explain a given BEHAVIOR. When discussing a phobia, for example, a previously NEUTRAL STIMULUS may become a CONDITIONED STIMULUS through PAIRING with the UNCONDITIONED STIMULUS. For example, a doctor may become a CONDITIONED STIMULUS eliciting severe fear in a child because she has been paired with the UNCONDITIONED STIMULUS of a painful needle prick. The phobia is then maintained, however, through an OPERANT CONDITIONING arrangement. In this latter case, anxiety is maintained through NEGATIVE REINFORCEMENT, with anxiety being reduced as an individual AVOIDS the phobic stimulus. For example, when the child now sees the doctor's office or the doctor, the fear is reduced by running away.

UNCONDITIONAL POSITIVE REGARD: Not a term used in ABA, per se, it refers to the belief that we should value all people and that this value should be independent from what people actually do. That is, we should love our children, spouses, neighbors, etc., even if their behavior leaves something to be desired. Nothing wrong with this! As Lenny Kravitz said "Let love rule!" Unfortunately, some individuals outside of ABA mistake the notion of unconditional positive regard to mean that all reinforcers should therefore NOT be contingent on the emission of certain behaviors. Rather, they believe that reinforcers should be given just for the sake of making the recipient "feel the love" (experience the unconditional positive regard). A large number of research studies in behavior analysis, however, have shown that learning of appropriate skills is much less likely if reinforcement is delivered predominantly in this NONCONTINGENT manner, rather than CONTINGENT upon the emission of appropriate behavior. For example, a child who has just misbehaved may become confused if he receives a hug from a parent who wishes to show the child "unconditional positive regard." The child may wonder if the misbehavior is something the parent approves of. "It must be good to misbehave since I got a hug!" Obviously this tactic can lead to a great many problems. In contrast to this, one of the major tenets of ABA is to consistently "catch a child being good" by providing hugs, praise, high-fives, privileges, etc. In this way, the child still "feels the love," but also learns appropriate skills and the relationship between behavior and consequences. Read Skinner's *Walden Two* to further examine this distinction.

UNCONDITIONED RESPONSE: Generally used in terms of CLASSICAL CONDITIONING, this is a response to the UNCONDITIONED stimulus. Generally speaking, learning is not required for this response to occur, it is a reflex in response to the presentation of the UNCONDITIONED STIMULUS. For example, a loud sound behind you is likely to elicit the UNCONDITIONED RESPONSE of being startled. Originally, this was called an "unconditional" response, meaning not dependent on any other factors. See UNCONDITIONED STIMULUS for elaboration.

UNCONDITIONED STIMULUS: Generally used in terms of CLASSICAL CONDITIONING, this is a stimulus that leads to a response without any teaching or training. Originally, this was called an "unconditional" stimulus, meaning not dependent on any other factors. Sometimes used in the context of a reflex relation, for example the relationship between an unconditioned stimulus (food) and an unconditioned response (salivation).

VARIABILITY: Refers to the degree of differences in behavior EMITTED by the individual. This can occur naturally, as an individual engages in a variety of exploratory or trial and error responses. This is also one of the more important elements of the EXTINCTION BURST when considering SHAPING procedures. During an EXTINCTION BURST, different responses are emitted, and one of these variations may be a closer APPROXIMATION to a TARGET BEHAVIOR one is trying to teach and should be reinforced. Conversely, inappropriate behavior may burst as well, and it is important to avoid reinforcing any of these variations (see EXTINCTION BURST). Note: this term is also used in the analysis of graphs to describe the RANGE of behavior around some central value. For example, a child may emit a mean of 12 social initiations per day, with a range of 5-17 initiations over multiple days.

VARIABLE INTERVAL SCHEDULE OF REINFORCEMENT: A particular type of INTERMITTENT SCHEDULE OF REINFORCEMENT wherein reinforcement is available for the first response that occurs after a changing interval has elapsed. A Variable Interval 2 minute schedule, for example, indicates that the first response that occurs after an average of two minutes have elapsed will be reinforced. Note that it does not matter how many responses occur during the interval itself, the only one that will be reinforced is the first one following the end of the interval, and the length of the interval will vary around some average value. This type of schedule generally leads to slow, steady responding, as the individual can never be sure when REINFORCEMENT will become available. For example, the behavior of asking "will you play with me?" is often reinforced on a variable interval scheduled of reinforcement by a busy, but well-meaning, caregiver.

VARIABLE RATIO SCHEDULE OF REINFORCEMENT: An intermittent schedule of reinforcement wherein reinforcement becomes available after an uncertain number of responses. The schedule is named for the average (arithmetic mean) number of responses needed for reinforcement (for example, VR 10 requires an average of 10 responses for reinforcement). This is among the most powerful schedules of reinforcement for encouraging rapid responding and providing RESISTANCE TO EXTINCTION. Within this schedule of reinforcement, the more responses emitted by the individual, the more likely it is that they will acquire reinforcement. For example, a child's nagging or whining behavior is often inadvertently reinforced by an adult on a variable ratio schedule when the adult "gives in" after the child has whined many times. Now guess what the child will do next time he is denied what he wants!

VERBAL BEHAVIOR: A book written by B. F. Skinner that describes a behavioral approach to language. It emphasizes that communication is a behavior that follows the same laws and principles as other forms of behavior. Within this book, Skinner introduced and described new terms to refer to language processes from a behavioral perspective (e.g., MANDS, TACTS, INTRAVERBALS, etc.). The book became the center of a controversy between linguist and social critic Noam Chomsky (who gave the book a poor review) and behavioral clinicians and philosophers (who felt Noam didn't truly understand the book). More recently, the term "verbal behavior" has also been informally applied to a teaching approach that emphasizes Skinner's analysis of language. A similar term, Applied Verbal Behavior, has been used by some to refer to this approach.

VICARIOUS REINFORCEMENT: A term often used in conjunction with MODELING, it refers to the reinforcement derived by observing reinforcement given to others. See work by Albert Bandura and colleagues, for example. For a good real world example, just look at the faces of parents when their children receive diplomas at graduation. For a disgraceful example, observe the behavior of many parents at children's athletic events.

VINELAND ADAPTIVE BEHAVIOR SCALE: Often called "the Vineland" for short, this is a popular assessment tool used to determine skill levels in the following areas: language, daily living skills, social skills, and gross and fine motor skills. Information is gathered regarding an individual by interviewing his or her parents or caregivers with a structured questionnaire.

VISUAL PROMPT: A CUE that is meant to be seen and that has behavior-altering effects. This may take the form, for example, of a culturally accepted symbol such as a "stop sign," or may take the form of something designed for an individual teaching program (e.g., holding up a red piece of construction paper while simultaneously asking a student to "touch red").   This can also be a MODEL or DISCRIMINATIVE STIMULUS. Also see PROMPT.

WALDEN TWO: A novel written by B. F. Skinner. In the utopian literature tradition, it describes a community that is organized according to applied behavior analytic principles. Depending on the critic, the book was described either as a wonderful vision of the future (utopia), or as an Orwellian nightmare (dystopia). Within ABA circles, the book is obviously considered a utopia and has been the basis for actual communities such as Los Horcones, Mexico.

WATSON, J. B.: John Watson was a psychologist and writer in the first half of the 20th century. His writings on behaviorism were a source of inspiration for Skinner and future behaviorists.

References and Suggested Reading

Azrin, N., & Foxx, R. M. (1974). *Toilet training in less than a day.* New York: Pocket Books.

Bailey, J. S. (1991). Promoting freedom and dignity: A new agenda for behavior analysis. Paper presented at the annual convention of the Association for Behavior Analysis, May 1991.

Bijou, S. W. (1970). What psychology has to offer education- now. *Journal of Applied Behavior Analysis, 3,* 65-71.

Binder, C., & Watkins, C. L. (1989). Promoting effective instructional methods: Solutions to America's educational crisis. *Future Choices, 1*(3), 33-39.

Cameron, J., & Pierce, W. D. (1994). Reinforcement, reward, and intrinsic motivation: A meta-analysis. *Review of Educational Research, 64,* 363-423.

Carr, E. G., & Durand, V. M. (1985). Reducing behavior problems through functional communication training. *Journal of Applied Behavior Analysis, 18,* 111-126.

Carr, J. E., & Sidener, T. M. (2002). On the relation between applied behavior analysis and positive behavioral support. *The Behavior Analyst, 25,* 245-253.

Cohen, I. L. (1994). Artificial neural network analogues of learning in autism. *Biological Psychiatry, 36,* 5-20.

Cooper, J. O., Heron, T. E., & Heward, W. L. (1987). *Applied behavior analysis.* Toronto: Merrill Publishing.

Durand, V. M. (1990). *Severe behavior problems: A functional communication approach.* New York: The Guilford Press.

Eisenberger, R., & Cameron, J. (1996). Detrimental effects of reward: Reality or myth? *American Psychologist, 51*, 1153-1166.

Foxx, R. M. (1982). *Decreasing behaviors of persons with severe retardation and autism* Champaign, IL: Research Press.

Foxx, R. M. (1982). *Increasing behaviors of persons with severe retardation and autism* Champaign, IL: Research Press.

Freeman, S. K., & Drake, L. (1997). *Teach me language.* Langley, British Columbia: SKF Books.

Goetz, E. M., & Baer, D. M. (1974). Social control of form diversity and the emergence of new forms in children's blockbuilding. *Journal of Applied Behavior Analysis, 6*, 209-217.

Green, G. (1996). Evaluating claims about treatments for autism. In C. Maurice, G. Green, & S. C. Luce (Eds.) *Behavioral intervention for young children with autism* (pp. 15-28). Austin, TX: Pro-Ed.

Greer, R. D. (2002). *Designing teaching strategies: An applied behavior analysis systems approach* New York: Academic Press.

Keller, F. S. (1968). Good-bye teacher. *Journal of Applied Behavior Analysis, 1*, 79-89.

Keller, F. S., & Sherman, J. G. (1982). *The PSI handbook: Essays on personalized instruction* Lawrence, KS: TRI Publications.

Koegel, R. L., & Koegel, L. K. (1995). *Teaching children with autism: Strategies for initiating positive interactions and improving learning opportunities.* Baltimore: Brookes.

Lovaas, O. I. (1987). Behavioral treatment and normal educational and intellectual functioning in young autistic children. *Journal of Consulting and Clinical Psychology, 55*, 3-9.

Lovaas, O. I. (1981). *Teaching developmentally disabled children: The ME book.* Austin: Pro-Ed.

MacCorquodale, K. (1971). Behaviorism is a humanism. *The Humanist, 31*(2), 11-12.

Malott, R. W. (1989). The achievement of evasive goals: Control by rules describing contingencies that are not direct acting. In S. C. Hayes (Ed.), *Rule-governed behavior: Cognition, contingencies and instructional control* (pp. 269-322). New York: Plenum Press.

Malott, R. W. & Suarez-Trojan, E. W. (2003) *Principles of Behavior (5th ed), the textbook formerly known as elementary principles of behavior.* Upper Saddle River, NJ: Prentice Hall.

Maurice, C. (1993). *Let me hear your voice.* New York: Knopf.

Maurice, C., Green, G., & Luce, S. C. (1996). *Behavioral intervention for young children with autism.* Austin: Pro-Ed.

McClannahan, L. E., & Krantz, P. J. (1999). *Activity schedules for children with autism: Teaching independent behavior.* Bethesda, MD: Woodbine House.

Meichenbaum, D. (1977). *Cognitive behavior modification: An integrative approach.* New York: Plenum Publishing.

Needelman, M. (2000). My role as a related service provider at an ABA school for children with autism. In B. Newman, D. R. Reinecke, & L. Newman (Eds.), *Words from those who care: Further case studies of ABA with people with autism* (pp. 130-138). New York: Dove and Orca.

New York State Department of Health Early Intervention Program (1999). *Clinical practice guideline: Report of the recommendations, autism and pervasive developmental disorders*

Newman, B. (1999). *When everybody cares: Case studies of ABA with people with autism.* New York: Dove and Orca.

Newman, B. (1992). *The reluctant alliance: Behaviorism and humanism.* Buffalo, NY: Prometheus Books.

Newman, B., Buffington, D. M., Hemmes, N. S., & Rosen, D. (1997). Answering objections to self-management and related concepts. *Behavior and Social Issues, 6*(2), 85-95.

Newman, B., Needelman, M., Reinecke, D. R., & Robek, A. (2002). The effect of providing choices on skill acquisition and competing behavior of children with autism during discrete trial instruction. *Behavioral Interventions, 17,* 31-41.

Newman, B., Reinecke, D. R., Birch, S., & Blausten, F. G. (2002). *Graduated applied behavior analysis.* New York: Dove and Orca.

Newman, B., Reinecke, D. R., & Newman, L. (2000). *Words from those who care: Further case studies of ABA with people with autism.* New York: Dove and Orca.

Newman, B., Tuntigian, L., Ryan, C. S., & Reinecke, D. R. (1997). Self-management of a DRO procedure by three students with autism. *Behavioral Interventions, 12,* 149-156.

Page, T. J., Iwata, B. A., & Reid, D. H. (1982). Pyramidal training: A large-scale application with institutional staff. *Journal of Applied Behavior Analysis, 15,* 333-351.

Rappaport, M. F. (2001). Notes from the speech pathologist's office. In C. Maurice, G. Green & R. M. Foxx (Eds.), *Making a difference: Behavioral intervention for autism* (pp. 163-180). Austin, TX: Pro-Ed.

Reinecke, D. R., Newman, B., & Meinberg, D. (1999). Self-management of sharing in preschoolers with autism. *Education and Training in Mental Retardation, 34,* 312-317.

Sidman, M. (1989). *Coercion and its fallout.* Boston: Authors Cooperative.

Skinner, B. F. (1976). The ethics of helping people. *The Humanist, 36*(1), 7-11.

Skinner, B. F. (1974). *About behaviorism.* New York: Random House.

Skinner, B. F. (1972). Humanism and behaviorism. *The Humanist, 32*(4), 18-20.

Skinner, B. F. (1971). Humanistic behaviorism. *The Humanist, 31*(3), 35.

Skinner, B. F. (1953). *Science and human behavior.* New York: The Free Press.

Stokes, T. F., & Baer, D. M. (1977). An implicit technology of generalization. *Journal of Applied Behavior Analysis, 10,* 349-367.

Sundberg, M. L., & Partington, J. W. (1998). *Teaching language to children with autism or other developmental disabilities.* Pleasant Hill, CA: Behavior Analysts, Inc.

Van Houten, R., Axelrod, S., Bailey, J. S., Favell, J. E., Foxx, R. M., Iwata, B. A., & Lovaas, O. I. (1988). The right to effective behavioral treatment. *Journal of Applied Behavior Analysis, 21,* 381-384.

About the Authors

Bobby Newman is a Board Certified Behavior Analyst and licensed psychologist. Affectionately known as the Dark Overlord of Applied Behavior Analysis, his past books include *When Everybody Cares: Case Studies of ABA with People with Autism, Words From Those who Care, Graduated Applied Behavior Analysis, No Virtue in Accident* and *The Reluctant Alliance.* Bobby is a Past-President of the New York State Association for Behavior Analysis. He has consulted and designed programs for individuals of all ages diagnosed with autistic-spectrum disorders, all over the United States as well as Canada, Ireland, England and Northern Ireland. Dr. Newman has been honored for his work with individuals diagnosed with autistic-spectrum disorders by several parents' groups, and hosts a regular radio call-in program with the parents of the ELIJA foundation. He is Director of Training at AMAC and widely acknowledged as the sexiest behavior anlayst of all time.

Kenneth F. Reeve received his Ph.D. in Learning Processes, with a specialization in developmental disabilities, from the City University of New York. Currently the Chairperson of the Psychology Department at Caldwell College in New Jersey, Ken teaches both undergraduate and graduate courses in behavior analysis and learning, developmental disabilities, and research methodology. He has been an active researcher in the areas of concept learning, infant imitation and language, and applied behavior analysis and autism. Ken also serves as a research and staff training consultant on the use of ABA in the treatment of pervasive developmental disorders. He is happily married to one of the authors of this book.

Sharon A. Reeve received her Ph.D. in Learning Processes from the City University of New York and is a nationally Board Certified Behavior Analyst. Sharon is currently an Assistant Professor of Education at Caldwell College in New Jersey where she is also the coordinator of the Special Education Teaching Certification Program. Over the past ten years, she has served as a director, staff trainer, and parent trainer for several schools and agencies serving children with autism, both in New Jersey and New York. In addition, Sharon maintains a private practice for children with autism and serves as a consultant for early intervention agencies and school districts. She regularly publishes and presents at professional conferences in behavior analysis and autism.

Carolyn S. Ryan is a Board Certified Behavior Analyst. Carolyn received a Bachelor of Arts in Psychology and Philosophy at Queens College, a Master of Arts in Psychology at Queens College, and a Master of Philosophy at the Graduate Center of the City University of New York, CUNY. She is completing her doctoral requirements in the Learning Processes subprogram in Psychology through the Graduate Center, CUNY. Carolyn teaches in the Psychology Department at Queens College, CUNY and works as a behavior analyst and an inclusion coordinator in mainstream and inclusion classrooms in various school settings. She conducts family and staff training sessions and workshops in topics ranging from inclusion to training self-care skills. Carolyn has worked with children and adults with developmental disabilities in data-based applied behavior analytic programs for the past 13 years. She has been employed through several agencies, schools, and school districts as a director, teacher, staff trainer, parent trainer, and behavioral consultant serving children with developmental disabilities and their families in the New York metropolitan area. She is the author and co-author of several articles in journals dedicated to Applied Behavior Analysis. Carolyn has made numerous presentations of her research at local, state, national, and international conferences.

The training materials supplementing *Behaviorspeak* were prepared with support from the Moody's Institute for Applied Research on Autism and Developmental Disabilities. The Institute is funded by The Moody's Foundation, a charitable foundation established by Moody's Corporation (NYSE: MCO, www.moodys.com) and is headquartered at AMAC, 25 West 17th Street, New York, NY 10011 (www.amac.org)

Our wonderful cover was once again designed for us by the great folks at Lounge Lizard Worldwide. Lounge Lizard is a full service advertising agency based in Great River, NY specializing in online and offline marketing. Thanks to Ken Braun and Sharon Sexton-Braun.   See   more   examples   of   their   great   work   at www.loungelizard.com